POST-PARKLAND:
ARE WE MISSING THE MARK?

Adam Salomon

*In memory of those whose lives have
been needlessly taken from us too soon.*

CONTENTS

FAILURES OF EPIC PROPORTIONS

People love narratives, and why not? They help us cope with a sudden tragedy when the pieces of the puzzle are either missing, hard to comprehend or even when we find it hard to face facts. Here we stand looking down the barrel of days gone by, salt in our still-healing wounds, questioning things we could have done, should have done or would have done had we not let narratives get in the way. But in trying to understand school shootings and how to move forward in their wake, are we missing the mark?

What follows will not be popular among Republicans, nor should it be. Likewise, it will not be popular among Democrats, nor should it be. But it needs to be said to serve as a voice of reason in the aftermath of an event that somehow divided us when it should have brought each and every one of us together with the goal of keeping our children safe.

The story begins in February 1996 when Barry Loukaitis, a 9th grade student who was continuously teased, arrived at Frontier Junior High in Moses Lake, Washington dressed in black and armed with a rifle gun. By the end of this school rampage, two students and a teacher had lost their lives. As unfavorable and vile as this shooting seemed at the time, it was only the beginning.

Two fatal shootings occurred in 1997. In October, Luke Woodham, then 16, killed his mother, went to his high school in Pearl, Mississippi with a gun, and shot nine students. Two of them died during the rampage. Two months later, during the holiday season, three students were killed and five injured, as a Michael Carneal, 14, brought a gun to a West Paducah, Kentucky school and opened fire in the hallway.

In March 1998, the death toll reached five during a shooting in Jonesboro, Arkansas. The shooting occurred when Andrew Golden, 11, and Mitchell Johnson, 13, pulled the fire alarm and waited in a nearby woods for the student population to make their way out of the building. Once they had a clear view of the students, they opened fire and claimed the lives of four girls and a teacher. Three other shootings occurred that year, including a one at a Fayetteville, Tennessee high school parking lot on May 19th. However, only two days later in Springfield, Oregon, two teenagers were killed and more than 20 injured when Kip Kinkel, then 15, opened fire at his high school. In addition, Kip's parents were found dead at their home.

There aren't always warning signs before such an event takes place. Within these school shootings, only three of the killers showed signs of aggression beforehand. Barry Loukaitis, who opened fire at his school in Moses Lake, Washington, wrote poetry about killing with the "ruthlessness of a machine" weeks before the incident. Kip Kinkel, who murdered his parents, then some students at his school in Springfield, Oregon, told a class that he dreamed of becoming a killer. Finally, Mitchell Johnson, the gunman at Jonesboro, became more aggressive in nature after his parents' divorce in 1994.

We questioned the mental health of the individuals involved but did nothing. We even accepted our findings as "normal." In fact, Scott Johnson, Mitchell's father, stated, "He started talking back and always pushed the limits. Mitchell saw a therapist on one occasion after the divorce." However, his mother, Gretchen, asserted, "...A therapist for what? This is a little boy who played football and basketball and loved school."

All of this happened before 1999, the year Eric Harris and Dylan Klebold attacked Columbine High School in Littleton, Colorado. Columbine ripped open the wounds of those still healing and exposed a fear we never thought possible. Harris and Klebold entered Columbine High School in Littleton, Colorado armed with several guns, explosives and knives and murdered 12 students and one teacher. They injured 21 additional people, and three more were injured while attempting to escape the school. After exchanging gunfire with responding police officers, the pair committed suicide. The blame game started, and heavy metal musician Marilyn Manson seemed to find himself directly in the crosshairs of social controversy.[1]

Eric Johns, a member of the now-defunct metal band Simple Aggression[2], was quick to defend Manson at the time, "Perhaps the reasons for such tragedies are right under all our noses and we just don't want to see it," he said in an interview. "We don't want to believe that the society we raise our children in is somehow flawed." The "Motor City Madman" Ted Nugent, an avid gun enthusiast, chimed in during an interview with *Metal Edge Magazine* following the attack:

> I think Marilyn Manson and the bloody video games are silly and inconsequential — if parents give guidance. If parents spy and hover and probe and guide and direct and manage. In the absence of any real parenting, Marilyn Manson and the recent video games and movies all of a sudden mean something.

Jaysinn, a member of the Kentucky-based band Crush, wanted to know:

> Why didn't anyone show them some attention before this? Is this what one has to do to get some attention? If it is true that the music did play a part in this, how can the parents be so

disconnected with their children that they aren't aware that they have a hate-filled website, making bombs, or planning the mass-murder of their peers?

Years passed, and many other shootings occurred, including one at Virginia Polytechnic Institute[3] in 2007 by Seung-Hui Cho, 23, who went on to kill 32 people with pistols, including a Glock 19 and Walther P22, before taking his own life. Like many before him, Cho began showing signs of mental instability during his adolescence, talking about suicide and murder during therapy sessions. However, the Virginia Tech professors who did take the time to notice Cho's troubles "ended up doing little more than coddling him — rewarding his most troubling writing with grades of B and even A," reported the *Washington Post*.[4]

Just a few years later on December 14, 2012 in Newtown, Connecticut, 20-year-old Adam Lanza fatally shot 20 children between six and seven years old, as well as six adult staff members at Sandy Hook Elementary. Prior to driving to the school, he shot and killed his mother. As first responders arrived at the scene, Lanza committed suicide by shooting himself in the head.

The shooting prompted renewed debate about gun control in the United States, including proposals for making the background-check system universal, and for new federal and state gun legislation banning the sale and manufacture of certain types of semi-automatic firearms and magazines with more than ten rounds of ammunition.

Ultimately, very little was done in the wake of Sandy Hook. The calls following the attack during a Las Vegas country music festival on October 1, 2017 were no different, especially after a heavy arsenal was found in gunman Stephen Paddock's Mandalay Bay hotel room. Still, federal lawmakers failed to act.

WHAT MAKES PARKLAND DIFFERENT?

Fast-forward to February 14th, 2018 in the Parkland section of Coral Springs, Florida, when Nikolas Cruz entered Marjory Stoneman Douglas High School armed with an AR-15, murdered 17 students and left 17 others injured. When the issue of stronger gun control came up in the media, the high school students in Parkland jumped as if on command and issued tear-filled pleas while expressing anger and disgust at the NRA and President Donald Trump. While at an anti-gun rally during the days that followed, Stoneman Douglas High student Emma Gonzalez simply called, "B.S."[5] toward the organization known for their political clout and a president everyone loves to hate as tears streamed down her face.

Their anger is 100 percent justified, but given the facts that have emerged in Parkland's wake, are they misguided this time around? Like many prior massacres on school grounds, there were warning signs — many of them. "Cruz had received mental health treatment but stopped going to a clinic," Broward Mayor Beam Furr, a former teacher, told CNN and NPR. "We missed the signs. We should have seen some of the signs."

His social media posts showed his love of weaponry. In some of his images, he sported dark bandanas over his face and beanies and baseball caps on his head. In one post, he wielded knives between his fingers as if they were claws. In another, he showed off a small black handgun. Cruz even appeared to have left an ominous comment on a Mississippi man's YouTube channel in September. Ben Bennight, a Gulfport bail bondsman who goes by "Ben the Bondsman" on YouTube, said in a video that he spoke to FBI field agents in Mississippi back in September about a comment left on one of his videos by someone with the username "nikolas cruz."

"I'm going to be a professional school shooter," the commenter wrote.

On January 5th, the FBI received a call on a tip line from a person close to Nikolas Cruz. The caller provided information on "Cruz's gun ownership, desire to kill people, erratic behavior and disturbing social media posts, as well as the potential of him conducting a school shooting," the FBI said.[6]

Cruz even had a tortured history at Marjory Stoneman Douglas High, where he had been suspended for fights and having ammunition in his backpack. He was later expelled for "disciplinary reasons," and was re-enrolled at a Broward school for at-risk youths. The family who took him in immediately after his mother passed away November 1st told police he had threatened others with a gun months before the Parkland attack, records show.[7] But according to NPR, the school system, led by Superintendent Robert Runcie, who worked alongside former Education Secretary Arne Duncan in the Chicago Public Schools, overhauled its policies and implemented the Promise Program to reduce the number of children going into the juvenile justice system and curb what is known as the "school-to-prison" pipeline.

Under the program non-violent misdemeanors would be handled by schools instead of the police. Although the newly-implemented system helped many students, proper authorities were never notified of Cruz's actions and comments. According to a *USA Today* article, the Broward County sheriff's office received 18 calls about Cruz's violence, threats and guns between 2008 and 2017, including concerns that he "planned to shoot up the school."[8]

The warnings, made by concerned people close to Cruz, came in phone calls to the Broward County Sheriff's office. At least five callers mentioned concerns over his access to weapons, but none of the warnings led to any direct intervention. In April 2016, an unidentified caller told police that Cruz had been collecting guns and knives. The caller was "concerned (Cruz) would kill himself one day and believes he could be a 'school shooter in the making.'" A second cousin even asked police to take away Cruz's guns after his mother died. "Nikolas is reported to have rifles, and it is requested that (deputies) recover these weapons," the dispatcher noted from one of the calls.

To make matters worse, the *Florida Sun-Sentinel* reported that instead of rushing in, several Broward sheriff's deputies waited outside the high school while Cruz went on his rampage, according to other officers on the scene.[9] These allegations emerged one day after another deputy, assigned as a school guard, resigned for also failing to enter the building. In all, at least three deputies waited outside, including School Resource Officer Scot Peterson.[10]

Two additional deputies are being investigated over whether they mishandled warnings about Cruz in the months before the shooting. The FBI has admitted it failed to investigate similar claims, and the Florida Department of Children & Families, which looked into concerns about Cruz, concluded that he was no risk to himself or others.

While Emma Gonzalez,[11] David Hogg,[12] Cameron Kasky, Jaclyn Corin and Alex Wind have led students nationwide to walkout of schools in favor of stronger gun control legislation, are their calls of "Enough is enough"[13] missing the mark? Perhaps not given the number of school shootings dating back to 1996. But they do seem extremely misguided and even disingenuous given the long series of failures that have come to surface in Parkland's wake.[14]

The narrative of "more gun control" just doesn't seem to fit the bill this time around. Andrew Pollack, whose 18-year-old daughter Meadow was shot nine times, said during a listening session with President Trump that he wouldn't rest until students are protected from future shootings:

> I am here because my daughter has no voice. She was taken from us. This shouldn't happen. We need to come together as a country and protect our children. Not think about different laws. Not as different parties. We go to the airport, I can't get on the plane with a bottle of water, but we leave some animal to walk into a classroom and shoot our children. We protect airports, we protect concerts, stadiums, embassies, the Department of Education that I walked in today that has a security guard in the elevator. One school shooting and we all should've fixed it. And I'm pissed because my daughter I'm not going to see again. She's not here. We all need to come together and come up with the right idea. It's not about gun laws right now. That's another fight, another battle. Let's fix the schools. Security, consultants, whatever you have to do. And then you can battle it out over gun laws.[15]

One of the attendees at that very same session didn't give his name but voiced support for arming teachers.[16] He said he lost his sister in the Florida shooting and told the president that the attack "could have been a very different situation" if teachers were trained to shoot:

Law enforcement takes seven, eight minutes to get there in an emergency. If a teacher or a security guard has a concealed license and a firearm on their waist they're able to easily stop the situation. Or the bad guy — I'll put it that way — would not even go near the school knowing that someone could fight back against them.

Patrick Neville, who survived the Columbine attack in 1999, agrees. In his current role as minority leader in the Colorado House of Representatives, he introduced a bill[17] that would allow people with a concealed carry permit to bring guns into K-12 schools, arguing that more kids would have survived the attack had teachers been armed:

> This act would allow every law-abiding citizen who holds a concealed carry permit, issued from their chief law enforcement officer, the right to carry concealed in order to defend themselves and most importantly our children from the worst-case scenarios. [18]

In order to move forward in a productive manner, we need to know where we are. Judging by the response of the media, our politicians and our students, we are simply at a crossroad without even asking questions over which path is best.

Do we heed the media's advice and let the words of Andrew Pollack fall on deaf ears, or do we follow in the controversial advice of Neville as someone who has lived through the ordeal? Is there a path in the middle that doesn't include arming teachers? Do we educate by telling our children, albeit in a flawed manner, that it is ok to be a free-thinker – as long as it conforms to the narrative being offered? Do we teach our children that one of the cornerstones of a free society is based on impulsive reactions rather than weighing pros, cons and repercussions? We've already seen the unintended consequences of our overreactions. Or do we think outside of the box by facing our fears, asking the questions that need to be asked and finally confronting a fatally flawed system that allowed a tragedy of this magnitude to occur?

Something is fundamentally and morally wrong with us if we allow our children to get killed while letting our emotions get in the way of rational thoughts like asking, "What happened?" We must not be afraid of asking important questions, even if they make us sound insensitive or even offensive. People's lives are at stake, and we must act as such. Are we afraid that the answers will present inconvenient truths that challenge our personal beliefs or biases? It certainly is shaping up that way, and we must not move forward until we get over this fear.

Questions about the Promise Program had been a source of frustration for district officials, as well as students and parents. Many felt that the program had been unfairly targeted by those against gun control, who preferred to focus on blundering by the district and the sheriff's office. But perhaps a good starting point in our quest for answers would be to examine the system itself and its many failures, especially since the Broward school district continues to offer false and misleading information about Nikolas Cruz.

The district has been in court battles against the release of school surveillance video and refused to issue any records regarding the shooting to the media which, according to the *Sun-Sentinel*, is a possible violation of the state's open-records law.[19] Superintendent Runcie has even blocked critics, including parents, from his Twitter account over questions pertaining to why the state commission on school safety was still waiting on the district to provide all of Cruz's disciplinary records. And most recently, Runcie has repeatedly claimed that Cruz was never involved in the Promise Program, despite records from other schools showing numerous connections.

"It would appear that the district is more interested in protecting their programs than they are the students and teachers in our schools," said Ryan Petty, whose 14-year-old daughter, Alaina, was killed by Cruz. "As a father, I would ask the district to please be completely transparent, so we can make sure this doesn't happen to any other children in any other schools in Florida."

Petty's concerns were proven correct when it was released that Nikolas Cruz was not only involved in the program after trashing a middle school bathroom in 2013, he also immediately violated it by skipping his three-day referral meetings. At that point, school policy stated that he should have been brought to court for a hearing before Judge Elijah Williams of the Broward County Delinquency Division, yet there is no record that it ever happened.[20]

Moreover, Cruz committed 58 infractions from 2012-17 at Westglades Middle School and Marjory Stoneman Douglas High School, even though he was enrolled in 2015 at another school at the time. In each instance, he received the same type of punishment — detention, an in-school suspension or out-of-school suspension for one to three days — which also went against district policy, creating a sense that he can do anything and get away with it.

According to Timothy Sternberg, a former assistant principal who helped run Promise from 2014-17, the problem wasn't that he was referred to the program. It was that the district failed to follow its own rules:

> There was simply a breakdown in communication. Normally, when a student doesn't complete the program, the district is supposed to tell the school, which then refers him to Judge Williams, but it doesn't appear that ever happened.

The way the Promise Program is supposed to work, the judge tries to convince the student to re-enter the program:

"They're sitting in front of the judge, and the judge tries to re-engage the student, telling them that, 'If you don't go to Promise, you have to go before the state's attorney and further criminal action will take place.'"

Even if Cruz refused to re-enter the program, he would have been on the radar of juvenile justice, giving substantial contact with law enforcement through warnings, police reports and even arrests. Based on Florida state law, this would have automatically barred him from purchasing a firearm.

DO WE REALLY NEED TO FIX WHAT ISN'T BROKEN?

States without the Promise Program have shown tremendous success in thwarting potential attacks thanks to ample communication between citizens and local and federal law enforcement agencies, yet in an effort to protect narratives and failed policies, we are overlooking those that work. One such system worked in Parkland's wake just a few miles from Sandy Hook in Waterbury, Connecticut where 21-year-old Christopher Roman was seen brandishing a black pistol in a video sent to a 17-year-old student of John F. Kennedy High School while saying he wanted to "shoot up" the school. Authorities were called, and he was arrested.[21]

The system worked in Virginia Beach, where upwards of 21 cases of school threats were being investigated, and as of February 23rd, at least nine arrests had been made.[22] Virginia Beach Public Schools Chief School Officer Rashard Wright said in the following plea to parents:

> We need your help. You talk to your children about using good judgement, and about being responsible digital citizens. In short, see something, please say something. The school

division has a number of resources for parents and students for the digital citizenship as part of our "be social be smart be safe" campaign.

"Threats against a school are not a joke, they are a crime. Threats against a school are not a misunderstanding, they are a crime," Virginia Beach's Commonwealth's Attorney Colin Stolle emphasized during a press conference. "The way we begin to stop school threats is at home, and that's where it is going to start. And it begins with parents being involved in what their kids are doing."

On April 4th, a teacher noticed that Christopher Salters, a student at South Fort Myers High School in Florida, was acting out of character and immediately notified school administrators.[23] The school's resource sheriff's deputy eventually found a handgun in Salters' backpack and arrested him after a brief chase.

"This behavior is totally unacceptable and will not be tolerated," said Undersheriff Carmine Marceno. "Sheriff Scott and I have made it our number one priority to ensure the safety of our children in every school in our county."

Ed Mathews, the Principal of South Fort Myers High School, sent the following voicemail to the district after the incident occurred:

> In order to provide open communication and ensure the safety of all students, I wanted to let you know that a student was arrested today for bringing a gun to school...Providing a safe and secure learning environment is of top priority for our school, and we take these incidents very seriously.

Salters' mother, Lakesha Robinson, had done everything but defend Christopher:

> I don't know about Chris taking that gun to school this morning. I took Chris to school this morning! If I knew Chris

has that gun this morning, I would have never! Never let him get out that car with that gun. I want my son to be locked up because I want my son to change. I'd rather see my son in jail than bury my son in a week.

In short, while many disenfranchised children want to test the system, there is no guarantee that each threat is credible, but we must act as if they are.

Such was the case in Everett, Washington during the days that followed, where the system also worked.[24] 18-year-old Joshua Alexander O'Connor's grandmother found credible writings in his journal about an up-coming attack at ACES Alternative High School and immediately called authorities.

Excerpts from the journal show the teen had been thinking about the shooting frequently and wanted to make it "infamous." O'Connor wrote in entries dated in January 2018: "I can't wait to walk into class and blow all those (expletives) away," and "I need to make this shooting/bombing infamous. I need to get the biggest fatality number I possible can."

He also wrote that he planned to use explosives: "I'm thinking about using pressure cooker bombs for Kamiak (easy to hide and will fit in a backpack) and the thermite/propane bomb for the MUK police distraction."

In an entry, April 19th is circled. Police alleged this date was important to O'Connor because the Oklahoma City bombing took place on April 19, 1995, and the Columbine High School attack took place on April 20, 1999. He even detailed step by step instructions on how he planned to carry out the attack, including the time of day.

IS IT REALLY ABOUT SCHOOL SAFETY?

Since the system has repeatedly proven itself to work nationwide, why are we falling for narratives that fail to keep our children safe *today*? Sure, we can discuss the issue of gun control and this time *make sure* it gets addressed in a timely manner. But there are still regions where weak links exist.

While Rhode Island governor Gina Raimondo aptly hailed the adoption of a "red flag" gun policy[25] designed to help keep guns away from those "who pose a danger to themselves and others," she turned a blind eye to the fact that 10 babies, all under 18-months old, have died in the past 26 months under the state's DCYF care.[26] Moreover, issues plaguing the state's 911 system have relatively went unnoticed.[27]

Representative Bob Lancia, a Republican, said the staffing problems have reached a critical level, forcing telecommunicators to put thousands of 911 calls on hold. He visited the E-911 center in January at the request of employees, who told him they are "at the end of their rope" and that the money collected by the state's E-911 cell phone fee doesn't even go to the Department of Emergency Management.

"They are overworked. They are stressed out. Worst of all, if there was an actual emergency, they are not manned enough to handle it," Lancia said.

To make matters worse, Michael O'Rielly, a member of the Federal Communications Commission, blasted the state for "effectively stealing" millions of dollars raised each year for the local emergency 911 system, calling the practice an "enormous deception."[28] He went on to say that Rhode Island had diverted more than $8 million, or 60 percent of the fees it collected for 911 and spent it on other budget items in the state's general fund.

There were no pickets at the state house calling for DCYF reforms, even after it became known that the department previously investigated one of the families involved.[29] And nobody walked out in protest over where their 911 cell phone fees are going, much less how these issues affect the safety of the state's residents. Nobody questioned what would happen if such attacks occurred in one of the state's 39 communities or how long it would take to get through to an operator. In the wake of Parkland, we should all be enraged that such weak links even exist.

Stories involving the safety and welfare of our children have been playing out nationwide for years, yet we are content in letting the media turn a blind eye in favor of a narrative that resonates. And for what? Could it be because 2018 is a mid-term election year, one where Democrats want to take back control of Washington and Republicans will do anything to keep it? Is it to advance the agenda of gun control at the risk of our children's safety?

This isn't about scoring points in what has become the spectator sport of politics, where Americans increasingly inhabit the filter bubbles of news and social media that correspond to their ideological affinities. Thanks to the Rachel Maddows and Rush Limbaughs, we have our separate "facts," often the result of what different media outlets consider relevant to their narrative.[30]

Contrary to what the media has offered, this is the time when we should all be embracing civil discourse as a means of searching for true answers. By engaging each other and having productive dialogues to address the issue of school violence, we enable ourselves to challenge our own beliefs and accept those of others, even if we disagree. Moreover, we give ourselves the clarity to see the irony in wanting to trust the government to find a solution when it was its own systemic failures that allowed many of the recent mass shootings to occur in the first place.

Sadly, we are not ready to have such dialogue. Emotions on both sides are still way too high, and a professor at Southern State Community College in Ohio even called for anti-gun activists to "storm the NRA headquarters" and "make sure there are no survivors."[31] He now claims it was a joke.

Though students involved in the national student walkout marking the one-month anniversary of the Parkland attack were mostly peaceful, the protests did spawn many concerns ranging from legal accusations of indoctrination to assaults. Ian Bashaw, a teacher at Ralph C. Mahar High School in Orange, Massachusetts, was interviewed by Hank Stolz on the *Talk of the Commonwealth* radio show[32] to discuss his school's walkout:

> They walked out as an act of solidarity saying, 'Enough is enough' and wanted to show they were standing with their fellow students in Florida. Something needs to be done to stop violence in schools, and this was a call to action to our elected officials. During lunch period that day, students who were 16 or older were given the opportunity to register to vote with the

idea that if congress isn't going to listen, then you vote and make the difference yourself.

As the conversation progressed, Stolz touched on some student backlash:

> Many school administrations and law enforcement were involved in the planning process of these events. And with them being involved, we've seen in other areas around us kids actually pushing back and rebelling a little bit, saying, "How can we have civil disobedience if the administration is involved and even condoning these walkouts?

Julianne Benzel, a high school history teacher in Rocklin, California was put on administration leave after wanting to discuss the politics behind the National School Walkout with her students.[33] According to KOVR-TV, Benzel says she never discouraged her students from participating in the walkout, but she did question whether it's appropriate for a school to support a protest against gun violence if they're not willing to support all protests.

"I didn't get any backlash from any of my students," she told the CBS affiliate. "They understood there cannot be a double-standard."

Benzel hopes the walkout prompts a bigger conversation, not just with second amendment gun rights, but first amendment free speech. "If you're going to allow students to walk up and get out of class without penalty then you have to allow any group of students that wants to protest," she said.

At Antioch High School near Nashville, Tennessee, students actually did turn violent.[34] Videos posted on social media show a group ripping down the American flag from a flagpole and stomping on it. Others showed students jumping onto patrol cars. Michelle Michaud, a spokesperson for Metro Nashville Schools explained:

Unfortunately, some students on our Antioch campus today chose to protest in ways that significantly disrupted school operations and threatened the safety and order for other students and staff within our school.

In Chicago, dozens of students from Simeon Career Academy saw the walkout as an opportunity to leave school grounds and opted to take part in a vandalism spree at a local Walmart.[35] Police said that between 40 and 60 students crossed the street and trashed parts of the store, knocking over product displays, yanking items off shelves, breaking packages and stealing small items like chips and candy, which surveillance from security and shoppers confirms. Simeon students who heard about the incident told the local Fox affiliate that they're angry a walkout intended to promote peace instead led to vandalism and violence.

Even worse, 17-year-old Christian Breault, a senior at Middleburgh Junior/Senior High School, in Middleburgh, New York, found himself physically attacked for supporting the Second Amendment when his school participated in the walkout.[36] After the walkout had ended, an assembly was held in the school, featuring local law enforcement and community leaders to talk to the students about school safety. Instead of safety, the assembly turned political, tensions rose, and Christian found himself targeted for his views. His father, Brian Breault, issued a statement via Facebook:

> Following the dismissal of the assembly Christian engaged in a conversation with other students who felt the assembly was not handled well. Christian expressed he felt the anti-NRA video was over the top and he found it offensive. Another student not involved in the conversation threatened him for his view on the video going as far as telling the school nurse that he would punch Christian in the face if he didn't stop

defending the NRA. The nurse told the student he could not say that, and no further action was taken.

Later that afternoon, Christian was assaulted by another student while he was leaving class and was punched twice in the side of the head before knocking his attacker to the floor. His attacker was suspended for three days, and even Christian was suspended for a day. Brian Breault spoke with the principal about the incident. According to Brian, the principal "was very combative and condescending to my concerns of the breakdown in keeping Christian safe."

The video shown during the assembly was CNN's "We Call B.S.," featuring Emma Gonzalez giving her impassioned speech in Ft. Lauderdale attacking the NRA and members of congress. No alternative perspectives were offered, and the video was approved by the principal. Middleburgh Schools Superintendent Brian Dunn offered the following apology:

> On Wednesday, March 14th, the Jr./Sr. High School held a school safety assembly for students. The purpose of the assembly was to give administrators and law enforcement the chance to speak with students regarding how the district handles school safety and answer any questions students may have had. During the assembly, a video was shown that changed the focus of the conversation from school safety to politics. This was not our desired outcome for the event, and we regret and sincerely apologize for that result.
>
> Conversations are happening across America about how we can keep students safe in school. No matter where you stand on this issue, we can all agree that student safety should be our top priority.

Given everything that has transpired during National School Walkout on March 14, 2018 and all the questions that have yet to be asked, one has to wonder if it is still *really* about the safety of our children.

THE AR-15: SEPARATING FACT FROM FICTION

Misinformation by gun control advocates has rapidly spread like wildfire, especially regarding calls to ban the AR-15, commonly misinterpreted as standing for "assault rifle" or "automatic rifle." But here are the facts, which both gun control activists and second amendment advocates alike might find eye-opening.

The ArmaLite Rifle-15 was designed by ArmaLite, Inc. in 1956, but the company sold its design and patents to Colt's Manufacturing, LLC in 1959. Five years later, Colt began selling its own version known as the Colt AR-15. After Colt's patents expired in 1977, an active marketplace emerged for other manufacturers to produce and sell their own AR-15 style rifles. Since then, the term "AR-15" has become a catchall that includes a variety of weapons that look and operate similarly, including the Remington Bushmaster, the Smith & Wesson M&P15 and the Springfield Armory Saint.

Determining the true effect of a ban is just about impossible because federal regulations prohibit the government from tracking guns.[37] 3.7 million rifles were manufactured in the United States in 2015, the most recent year for which the Bureau of Alcohol, Tobacco and Firearms has data available to the public.[38] Compared with pistols, such rifles are rarely used in shootings. According to FBI statistics, 374 people were murdered with any kind of rifle in 2016, whereas 7,105 were killed by a handgun.[39]

Will a ban work? In September 1994, such rifles were taken off shelves after President Bill Clinton signed a law banning what Congress dubbed "assault weapons." Prompted by a string of mass shootings, including one in 1989 in Stockton, California in which five children were killed and 32 wounded in a schoolyard, the legislation stopped production of civilian rifles like the AR-15. Along with the ban, the term "assault weapon" was introduced to the public.

The number of assault weapons recovered by the police in crimes and reported to the ATF dropped sharply after the ban was carried out, according to a Justice Department report.[40] But it stops short of directly tying the ban to a decrease in gun violence, and the ban's broader effect remains in dispute. Gun rights advocates say loopholes allowed for the sale of slightly modified versions throughout the ban. Its defenders cite law enforcement statistics showing a drop in the criminal use of automatic and semi-automatic weapons during that time.

Culturally, the ban did what marketers could not — in outlawing it, the government made the AR-15 that much more alluring. "If you want to sell something to an American, just tell him that he can't have it," said Mark Westrom, who owned ArmaLite.

AR-15's re-entered the gun market after the federal assault weapons ban expired in 2004 and were popularized by the rise of a video game culture in which shooting became an accessible form of entertainment. Children were shooting the AR-15's military equivalent in wartime video games,[41] and by 2016 there were an estimated 16 million firearms in circulation that politicians would deem "assault weapons."

The Giffords Law Center recently issued their Annual Gun Law Scorecard, citing correlations between a state's gun laws and its gun death rate.[42] Though the report fails to mention any methodology or even what the term "gun death rate" refers to (such as suicide, self-defense, police shootings, gang violence or murders), Florida is ranked among the worst with a rating of "F."

HASHTAGS, EXCLUSIONS AND NARRATIVES

This question may be a bitter pill for many to swallow, but how can one truthfully back the #ParklandStrong, #NeverAgain and #EnoughIsEnough movements in their current form when people like Parkland survivor and #NeverAgain supporter Kyle Kashuv feel excluded?[43]

"A lot of people in the movement, they view it as, 'You're with us or you're against us' — there's no middle ground," he explained. "So, either you support them on all of their policy ideas, or you're an enemy."

Sadly, he is not the only one with this sentiment. Ariana Klein and Colton Haab, both Parkland survivors, feel as if they're both being silenced. Klein told Fox News' Tucker Carlson:

> Our voices need to be heard, and he (Haab) should have been able to ask any question he had to ask. But, instead we have these networks that don't want us to give our real opinions, and they want us to further their own agendas. The whole point of the (CNN) town hall meeting was to hear the kids and hear what we had to say. [44]

Most importantly, since it seems as if school safety is prioritized second to pushing gun control legislation within these movements, at what point does any proposed legislation just become an overreaction based on the emotion of the day? Simple. It is when we cannot have an honest, open conversation to discuss ideas and solutions from different points of view.

To their credit, David Hogg, Emma Gonzalez and several other Stoneman Douglas students wanted to meet with members of congress and the senate during their stay in Washington for the March for Our Lives but claim they were denied because they didn't have appointments. While it is generally true that such arrangements are needed, they chose to lash out at legislators during their speeches instead of using their public forum to request in-person meetings. The fact that a 2,200-page omnibus spending bill was being voted on that weekend didn't fit their narrative.

#NeverAgain means just that. Pushing gun control legislation through at light speed based on emotion does not address the issue of school safety today in any way, shape or form. Given legislators only had 48 hours to read the massive spending bill,[45] it's highly unlikely they would have time to comprehend gun control measures before passing such reforms on principle alone. Moreover, any legislation would take years to have any positive effect – if even done right – with very little impact on school safety. This grave oversight only makes #EnoughIsEnough sound like a catchy campaign slogan during an election year.

Even though it might still be a touchy subject, let's have that open and honest discussion. Passing gun control legislation and ensuring school safety are two separate goals and must be treated as such.

Enacting strict gun laws that actually work will take time to implement if we are to do it right, and that is assuming they do work in the end. Even if we passed comprehensive gun reform today with absolutely no loopholes, our schools will still not be safe, nor will they ever be.

In April 2014, 20 students and a security officer at Franklin Regional Senior High School in Murrysville, Pennsylvania were either stabbed or slashed in an attack by 16-year-old Alex Hribal who came to school wielding two kitchen knives.[46] During the attack, those who tried to help victims put themselves in harm's way and ended up as victims. Four students were left in critical condition after the attacker was subdued by an assistant principal.

Authorities did not release a possible motive in the attack, but the district attorney said in court the teen made "statements when subdued by officials that he wanted to die."[47] Yet there were no calls for metal detectors or any other safety measures. Or if there were, they fell on deaf ears.

We could have learned a lot from Murrysville, as it took place only two short years after Sandy Hook. But we didn't. Instead, we find ourselves turning a blind eye to Andrew Pollack's calls for school safety and instead wanting to impulsively act on the emotional pleas of Emma Gonzalez and David Hogg who are making their nationwide media rounds as if to run for some kind of office. Hogg, who will be taking a "gap year" from college to work on midterm elections,[48] has even went so far as to say he will not return to school until new gun control law passes[49] and asked tourists to boycott Florida over spring break.[50]

Sadly, we've already missed the mark by heeding these calls, and our students' safety was put at risk yet again — in the wake of Parkland no less. But this time it barely made any ripples in the media, let alone the splash the hashtag movements needed if they are to be taken seriously in their current form.

On March 6, 2018, a teen drawn to ISIS brought a homemade bomb to Pine View High School in St. George, Utah and hid it in his backpack.[51] The school was evacuated only after a student noticed smoke coming from the bag. Additional charges are also pending against the teen, whose name police hadn't disclosed, for allegedly raising the Islamic State's flag on a pole at nearby Hurricane High School in February.

Luckily no one was hurt, and no damage was reported. Police did not describe the homemade bomb but said it had the potential to cause significant injury or death:

> Based on our investigation we can confirm this was a failed attempt to detonate a homemade explosive at the school. It was also determined that the male had been researching information and expressing interest in ISIS and promoting the organization.

Just two weeks later on March 20th, a student at Great Mills High School in Great Mills, Maryland, brought a handgun into the school and opened fire on fellow students, injuring a male student and 16-year-old Jaelynn Willey, who eventually succumbed to her injuries.[52] Only this time, the renewed calls for stricter gun control became less intense with each detail released.

The gunman turned out to be 17-year-old Austin Wyatt Rollins, who had a previous relationship with Willey. The shooting was over in a matter of seconds, thanks to the quick action of the school's sole resource officer, Blaine Gaskill. The two exchanged fire until Rollins was fatally shot.[53] St. Mary's County Sheriff Tim Cameron said of the incident:

> He responded exactly as we train our personnel to respond. This is what we train for, this is what we prepare for and this is what we pray that we never have to do. On this day, we

realized our worst nightmare – the notion of "it can't happen here" is no longer a notion.

On the same day as the Great Mills attack, there were still troubling events coming out of Marjory Stoneman High, even though the Florida school had been placed under the global microscope. News broke via the *Sun-Sentinel* that two students were arrested on weapons charges.[54] Jordan Salter, 18, was arrested following a conflict in the cafeteria in which she poured cereal on a male student's head after he asked her friend a sexually offensive question. When the boy leaned in close to Salter's face, she pulled a black, 2-inch knife from her bra and opened it.

The next arrest came just a few hours later when school authorities learned that Gavin Stricker, 16, had waved a knife on his school bus that morning. After being called into the school's office, a 9-inch knife was found in his backpack.

The third incident surfaced after screenshots of an unidentified sophomore's Snapchat account circulated around the school. It showed a boy posing with a gun in his waistband along with images of bullets. The photos were captioned with "catch me out here n----," and one referenced a student named "Josh," the sheriff's office said. The student was hospitalized for a mental health evaluation and told detectives that the firearm was a BB gun and the bullets belonged to his father. It was also reported that the student used the name "NickCruz" as his moniker for the online game Fortnite, in an ominous nod toward Nikolas Cruz.

These unsettling incidents came one day after Zachary Cruz, the 18-year-old brother of Nikolas and branded a threat by prosecutors, was arrested for trespassing on school grounds. But that wasn't all. A deputy was suspended for sleeping on the job after being caught by a student on the night of Zachary's arrest. The student notified a sergeant patrolling the school that Deputy Moises Carotti was "asleep in his patrol car," said Veda Coleman-Wright, a spokeswoman for the sheriff's office. The sergeant then knocked on Carotti's window to wake him up.

Perhaps the most troubling of all isn't even the lack of coverage by the media relating to the latest to come out of Parkland – it is the deafening silence by Emma Gonzalez and David Hogg on both the Maryland shooting *and* the developments coming out of their very own school.

Austin Rollins, the 17-year-old Great Mills shooter, was well below Maryland's 21-year age requirement to purchase or possess a handgun, according to the progressive Giffords Law Center.[55] Moreover, he used a 9 mm Glock to carry out the shooting, a weapon legal even in the most highly-regulated countries. In fact, based on the law center's own rankings, Maryland has the 6th strongest gun laws in the nation, earning them an overall grade of A-.

A second event occurred nearly two months later in another highly regulated state, but this time it barely made any news at all. On May 16th, 19-year-old Matthew Milby, a former student at Dixon High School in Dixon, Illinois, entered the school and fired several shots near the gymnasium. Mark Dallas, a 15-year police department veteran acting as the school's resource officer for the past five years, was quick to intervene, injuring Milby in the shoulder after a brief chase.

"From the angle I'm looking at right now, a lot of things went right today when a great many of them could have (gone) wrong," Dixon Mayor Liandro Arellano Jr. said. "Things could have gone much worse."[56]

A woman who identified herself as Milby's mother addressed reporters and said her son had been "very sad" for a very long time and added, "He was bullied and ostracized at school, and was beaten up in October."[57]

Officials initially described Milby as a former student, but the woman said Milby still attended Dixon High School, where he worked independently out of the principal's office. It was released the following day that the 9mm gun Milby used was in fact his mother's.

Authorities said students "did exactly as they were trained to do in such situations" and were "pleased to discover that students had barricaded themselves into classrooms by blocking doorways with chairs, desks and other furniture."

It should also be noted that the school resource officer position at Dixon High School was started by the Dixon Police Department in 2000 to help prevent school violence.

If the arguments by the media, Gonzalez and Hogg really were about student safety, these two incidents surely diminished it. The facts just didn't fit the narratives this time around.

Kyle Kashuv further explained this to Fox News during the March for Our Lives rally in Washington, D.C. on March 24th, which omitted calls for safety measures outside of background checks:

> I don't think what David Hogg is saying right now is true, and I don't think what he's doing is positive for the American people. If he really cared, he would sit down, and he would talk to legislators. He would get all aspects of the discussion, and then he would act. Guns aren't the issue. It's everything surrounding acquiring a weapon. It's people who are not mentally stable who can acquire a weapon. It's the police forces and agencies not giving all the information. I talked to so many marchers, and they don't have a clear-cut solution. And it pains me to see that the government is not being held accountable for their failure. I don't see anyone looking at the

FBI wondering why tips weren't followed through. I don't see anyone wondering why there were 78 reports to the Broward Sheriff's Office and nothing was done. How come this isn't being represented right now? How come we don't hear marchers and speakers talking about the subject? This is what's going to save American lives. People aren't asking these questions because it's hard to look at all the facts. They don't want to hear that guns aren't the issue. Intellectual honesty is in question here, as they're not holding a clear message point. I believe that they sincerely care about this issue. But the thing is they're branding it as stopping school violence, but in reality, it's an anti-gun march.[58]

After finding out the march was secured by the National Guard, Charlie Kirk, Founder and Executive Director of the conservative think tank Turning Point USA, echoed Kashuv's sentiments, "They're using armed guards for this whole thing, which I think is one of the greatest ironies of a gun control march."

Hunter Pollack came to Washington, D.C. to honor the memory of his sister Meadow at the march. Both he and his father Andrew have been very vocal about their support of increased school security measures, which he was prepared to speak about.[59] However, he was denied an invitation that morning. The event's organizers claimed he was scheduled to speak, even though no official list of speakers was ever made public.

"I feel that they don't really care about the victims' families," he said in a video posted to Facebook. "If they did, they would have let me speak. I don't know what this is about, but it's definitely not about the victims."

A Resources link on the march's official website even confirms the notion.[60] *AdAge*, a magazine publishing news and analysis for the marketing and media field, has designed posters for download and urges people to use them during future marches.[61] Even more troubling, the narrative has taken a turn from focusing on school safety to one using colorful language such as:

- "No More – Guns Over People"
- "Trigger change"
- "It's not a right"
- "Fuck guns"
- "NRA: Stop being dicks"
- "NRA punks, fuck off"
- "The man don't give a fuck"

One poster even depicts the GOP logo, an elephant, holding an AR-15 in its trunk aimed at the outline of a child.[62]

ARE NARRATIVES BASED ON GOOD INTENTIONS PUTTING OUR CHILDREN AT RISK?

While the hashtags and narratives are based on good intentions, there will be unintended consequences that can be minimized, if not alleviated, if we acknowledge them in the midst of the calls for greater gun control. While at the march, Stoneman Douglas student Delaney Tarr boldly stated, "This is a movement," as cheers erupted. "We cannot move on, and if we do, the NRA and those against us will win...We will take the big, and we will take the small. When they give us that inch – that bump stock ban – we will take a mile. We are not here for breadcrumbs."[63] While gun rights advocates were getting up in arms over her comments, she went on to clarify that was in reference to an assault weapons ban.

But what exactly is meant by a "ban on assault weapons?" The answer is subjective. Some people claim it is a weapon with a high magazine capacity that should only be used in the armed forces, and others believe it to be based on its shape. There are also those who say it could refer to *any* gun that kills people, according to *Campus*

Reform, who interviewed marchers in Washington, D.C.[64] Regardless of what it means to each individual, people just want them taken off the market.

"I think there should be more cops in schools, but I don't think that would be as helpful as just taking guns from those who shouldn't have them," a Maryland teen told *Reason*'s Robby Soave. "Certain guns, like AR-15s, shouldn't even be accessible to the public."[65]

Still, not everyone agrees that banning "assault-style weapons," whatever that means, will save lives in our schools, a notion bolstered by the fact that Columbine took place during the 1995-2004 ban. C.J. Westfall, known for his *Conservatarian* podcast show, set out to listen to random marchers' concerns and honestly discuss their solutions while attending Charleston, South Carolina's March for Our Lives at Riverfront Park on March 24th.[66] However, the first thing he noticed as he started filming was the high level of security. "This march," he said while observing the large crowd entering the park, "was advertised as being 'anti-gun.' And all these people are going through security to make sure none of them are armed. We're protected by people with guns here, but they won't protect our schools."

The first person he interviewed in the unedited video, which was not even paused during recording, was holding a sign that read, "Our grandchildren deserve safety." After learning about what the sign meant to its creator, Westfall asked if the gentleman heard about Maryland and what stopped the shooting.

"That man stopped him," the marcher said.

"The resource officer with the gun?" Westfall asked.

"That's debatable, and they're still investigating," the man responded.

The next person Westfall interviewed was holding a sign that read, "Ban assault weapons now" and identified herself as "Becky." Unaware that they had been banned since 1984, she strongly believed that we should ban automatic weapons due to their high magazine capacity. Moreover, she insisted that our schools *are* safe and that high capacity guns are the problem, despite conceding that knives and pistols could still be brought in. When asked what should be done, she simply said, "Ban assault weapons."

"Politics is symbolic," a voice suddenly called out. Westfall approached the man and asked what he meant. The marcher explained:

> It doesn't matter if there's going to be an absolute drop in violence. What matters is that the people elected should represent the people's voices. The symbolism behind a ban or a restriction or an increased age requirement is successful if you can just get people elected to represent the voices of the people.

Stunned at the lack of logic in this rationale, Westfall panned the camera toward himself and summarized his experience at the event:

> We have a good number of people who are following us around saying we should not talk to anybody and threatening to kick us out just for asking questions. There are people who really do believe differently, and I respect other people's opinions. If someone wants to believe differently than me I respect you. But today what we've seen is people just shouting us down for having different opinions.

Before turning the camera off, one young mother who overheard Westfall's interviews approached him and asked what he thought would stop school shootings. "Armed officers on premises," he answered before asking if she heard about how the Maryland shooting concluded.

The marcher quickly deflected the question, not wanting to admit a "good guy with a gun" ended it and said that didn't work in Parkland. Despite Westfall explaining the timeline of events at Stoneman Douglas, she still adamantly denied that officers were told to stand down. When asked why armed resource officers would be a bad solution, she offered the following:

> Guns were created to kill, not protect. So, when you take killing machines in school and put them around people who don't have any idea how to use them, the number of children who misfire weapons and kill themselves or other students is very high...I'm very much in favor of (New York City Mayor) Bill De Blasio's policies.

She then walked off in a huff, seemingly unaware that resource officers are highly trained to quickly assess situations and act accordingly.

The marcher was referring to De Blasio's plans to remove all police presence from the city's public schools, a move that had many concerned New York City parents up in arms.[67]

"My colleagues think it's outrageous — and really stupid," teacher Arthur Goldstein said. "We're not enthusiastic about arming teachers, but we liked having a cop around."

Under the mayor's new policy, unarmed school safety agents would be stationed at all schools, and officers would still visit while patrolling the neighborhood.

During Rhode Island's March for Our Lives event, signs with slogans such as "Protect kids, not guns," 'I want to worry about my GPA, not my life," "My child is more important than your gun," "My grandkids deserve safe schools" and "Grandma for gun control" could be seen among the hundreds gathered on the state house lawn in Providence.

"As a mother, I'm sick of it," said Governor Gina Raimondo during a short speech. "As a governor, I'm sick of it. As a Rhode Islander, I'm sick of it, and it's time."[68]

Judging by Raimondo's stance on school safety, one has to wonder what exactly it is time for. Like Mayor De Blasio, Raimondo has been a critic of having armed resource officers in the state's schools.

Josh Block, a spokesman for the governor, released the following statement:

> Governor Raimondo believes that schools should be places of learning, not prisons, and she also believes the answer to gun violence is not more guns in our schools. We need a statewide ban on assault weapons and high-capacity magazines, and we need to ensure every school has secure windows, doors that lock, and intercom systems that work.[69]

While a good portion of the state's residents seem to echo her sentiments, believing the issue centers around guns, they have turned a blind eye to the safety and security of the schools themselves, which are now riddled with problems thanks to decades of neglect. With issues ranging from leaky ceilings, drafty walls and windows and even mold, the implementation of secure windows and doors or even metal detectors seem like a lofty goal.

However, Raimondo quickly changed her tune following the Maryland school shooting, saying armed school resource officers should be determined by each community:

> We need to work within each community to determine how best to keep students safe. If local communities determine that

school resource officers are an appropriate part of their security plans, it is absolutely critical that the SROs get the training that's necessary to respond to an emergency.

Perhaps the most shocking comments about arming school resource officers have come out of the very state where one such officer stopped a shooting. Baltimore Mayor Catherine Pugh issued the following statement:

> I'm not interested in having police officers with guns inside our schools. I'm more interested in our schools having the supplies, the kind of technology, that our young people need in order to learn, and to be productive members of our community.[70]

Republican Del. Pat McDonough, now running for Baltimore County Executive, said, "I don't know what the point is in having them unarmed. What happens if there is an armed intruder, shout them down? It doesn't make any sense."

Officer Don Bridges, president of the National Association of School Resource Officers (NASRO), said about the concept of arming SROs:

> How crucial is it? It is very, very critical, as we move closer to making schools less of a soft target. You send that message by having that patrol car parked out front. That message is there is a police officer in that building.

Does Pugh really believe her own comments? It's all in how one interprets her actions. Many of Baltimore's schools are without heat and hot water due to systems that have never been updated. Yet, the mayor heeded the calls of student safety by dedicating as much as $100,000 of taxpayer money to provide 60 school buses, free t-shirts and boxed lunches for roughly 3,000 students to attend the March for Our Lives in Washington.[71]

Perhaps the most shocking, David Hogg's own comments seem to suggest that he is on a more personal agenda of banning firearms than one of making a positive impact or ensuring the safety of our nation's youth. As a journalism student, he stated on CBS' *39 Days* documentary, "I wanted to get as much video and as many interviews as I could."

What he now supports may actually put our nation's youth in harm's way.[72] He took to the airwaves and appeared at a gun control forum with Axios's Mike Allen, where he complained about some new rules to promote security at Stoneman Douglas High School, including a policy that would require students to wear clear backpacks:

> I think after we come back from spring break, they are requiring all of us to have clear backpacks. One of the other important things to realize is many students want their privacy. There are many, for example, females in our school that when they go through their menstrual cycle, they don't want people to see their tampons and stuff. It's unnecessary, it's embarrassing for a lot of the students and it makes them feel isolated and separated from the rest of American school culture where they're having essentially their First Amendment rights infringed upon because they can't freely wear whatever backpack they want regardless of what it is. It has to be a clear backpack. What we should have is just more policies that make sure that these students are feeling safe and secure in their schools and not like they're being fought against like it's a prison.

Unfortunately, Hogg never elaborated on what those policies should entail and instead railed against the increased security presence:

When you have all these new police officers and resource officers coming into schools, what I'm worried is going to happen is we're going to increase the school-to-prison pipeline.

We now find ourselves heeding the calls of banning bump stocks and weapons like the AR-15 and will stop at nothing to achieve those goals, even if they mean putting our children in harm's way. While Hogg, along with fellow classmates Emma Gonzalez, Cameron Kasky, Jaclyn Corin and Alex Wind implore voters to take to the polls and elect school committee personnel and lawmakers who favor such measures and then some, they may in fact be urging constituencies to elect those who support the very policies that allowed Parkland to happen in the first place. This potentially dangerous and counter-productive narrative has been the only one garnering nationwide media attention. It took center-stage during the school walkouts, and it was a primary focus of the March for Our Lives movements across the country, leaving little room for other topics of discussion such as actual safety measures and the Promise Program.

The only exception can be found coming from some of the Stoneman Douglas students themselves, who claim the "student activists" don't speak for them. An unnamed faculty member commented during Dana Loesch's SiriusXM radio show:

> I've had some students approach me privately to talk to me about it. What is interesting is none of the student activists were ever in any danger during this whole thing...none of them except Samantha Fuentes. I have students in my class that were shot, but you don't see them. They have the most personal experience of anyone. A lot of my students have told me word for word as well as paraphrasing that these kids don't speak for all students.

The faculty member also noted the constant spotlight being cast on the activists is not helping matters much:

> Every single day since we've come back to school, I have kids out in the hall crying because of the emotional toll that it's taken, and we haven't started to heal yet, because we're in the news every single day.[73]

The sentiments C.J. Westfall encountered were not limited to Charleston, South Carolina. Westfall, along with Stoneman Douglas student Kyle Kashuv and Hunter Pollack, whose sister Meadow was among the 17 killed, are wrongfully placed in the "against us" category simply for asking questions that go against the media narratives.

As well-intentioned as the calls of Bill De Blasio, Gina Raimondo, Catherine Pugh and even David Hogg may have been to keep armed resource officers out of our schools, they are absolutely disingenuous given that actual safety policies either aren't even an after-thought in this discussion or are frowned upon. When specifically asked about metal detectors during an interview with WPRO radio talk show host Gene Valicenti, Raimondo responded, "I don't want our schools to become prisons, nor should they be," before doubling down on the notion that stricter gun control is the solution that will keep children safe.

What's even more disturbing is that gun control advocates have turned a blind eye to law enforcement reforms and proven systems in favor of platforms that sound good in theory. Raimondo and her office are protected by the very same measures she doesn't want to see in our schools, yet many don't want to see the irony in her stance against protective measures.

We proudly display signs in front of our houses and places of business to proclaim they are protected by an alarm system as a way of deterring criminals. According to Safewise, an organization that provides resources to create safe homes and communities, thieves generally look for homes that are easy to enter with quick routes of escape, which security systems don't allow.[74]

Yet many gun control advocates engage in the feel-good measure of creating "gun-free zones" as a means of making people believe they are safe. Communities have even gone so far as prominently displaying such signs in front of schools and other public spaces. But much like presenting alarm signs would-be criminals know are fake, this too has a dark and potentially grave downside.

Since at least 1950, over 98 percent of mass shootings in America have taken place where the public is banned from carrying a firearm, based on Crime Prevention Research Center's findings.[75] One such incident occurred at a Waffle House restaurant in Antioch, Tennessee, two months after Parkland, where 29-year-old Travis Reinking murdered four patrons. Waffle House is one of the many businesses that prohibit firearms.[76]

In an effort to "improve safety," the school committee in one Rhode Island community approved a resolution that supports state legislation to designate schools as "gun-free zones." The measure supports legislative efforts to ban firearms on school grounds, except by "peace officers,"[77] a term that by state law describes anyone from police officers to workers compensation and auto theft investigators. Fire marshals are even included, but "school resource officers" or the like are nowhere to be found.[78] And that is perfectly fine with Raimondo, who is a proud proponent of gun-free zones.

Perhaps the most shocking thing is some of the messages she and others support are echoed in *AdAge*'s March for Our Lives posters, which could be so misconstrued that they would be better at coaxing a deranged individual to enter an unprotected, "gun-free" school filled of kids who are being taught they are victims rather than serving as a wakeup call for protective measures. Here is just a sample of such messages we can expect to see at future marches:

- "Don't let them (children) become targets"
- "Killing kids isn't cool"
- "Stop shooting our children"
- "Classrooms are not a shooting range"
- "Schools – not warzones"
- "I hope to survive school"
- "Your kid could be next"
- "Not in our school"

One even depicts a hand holding a gun with the word "Me" inside of it, aimed directly at the outline of a child wearing a backpack surrounding the words "Your child." The headline reads, "What if?"[79]

With the proper safety protocols in place, such as RFID badges to keep unauthorized individuals out, communication between law enforcement agencies, metal detectors or even armed resource officers, there should not be a "what if." Yet, from Virginia Tech to a movie theater in Colorado to schools nationwide, such mass shootings are usually in venues declaring themselves gun-free zones. Given everything we've seen happen across the country, including the conclusion of the Maryland attack, are we *really* to believe that focusing on a weapons ban above all else will actually keep our schools from becoming soft targets *today*? Or are we just kidding ourselves into a false sense of security? Whatever opinion one may have regarding regulations or a ban at any level, they must not be mistaken as being the absolute solution.

IF GUN CONTROL IS SO GREAT, WHY HAS IT FAILED?

Overall, do Emma Gonzalez and David Hogg have valid points, or are they misguided? According to the Pew Research Center, only 12 percent of Americans believe the gun crime rate is lower today than it was in 1993; 56 percent believe it's higher.[80] The same study, based on stats from the Centers for Disease Control, concluded that the rate of U.S. gun violence has fallen dramatically since 1993:

> Compared with 1993, the peak of U.S. gun homicides, the firearm homicide rate was 49 percent lower in 2010, and there were fewer deaths, even though the nation's population grew. The victimization rate for other violent crimes with a firearm — assaults, robberies and sex crimes — was 75 percent lower in 2011 than in 1993.[81]

Moreover, a 2016 *Telegraph* report — based on findings in the Small Arms Survey and the 2012 Congressional Research Service Report — found the U.S. ranked number one in the world in per-capita gun ownership, but the U.S. did not even crack the top 10 when it came to firearm-related deaths.[82]

In 1998, Massachusetts passed what was hailed as the toughest gun control legislation in the country.[83] It banned semi-automatic "assault" weapons, imposed strict new licensing rules, prohibited anyone convicted of a violent crime or drug trafficking from ever carrying or owning a gun and enacted severe penalties for storing guns unlocked.[84] Within four years, the number of active gun licenses in the state had plummeted. There were nearly 1.5 million active gun licenses in Massachusetts in 1998, the *AP* reported.[85] In June (2002), that number was down to just 200,000.

The law that was tough on legal gun owners had a completely different effect on criminals. The *Boston Globe* reported that in 2011, the state recorded 122 murders committed with firearms, "a striking increase from the 65 in 1998."[86] Other crimes rose as well. Between 1998 and 2011, robbery with firearms climbed 20.7 percent, and aggravated assaults jumped 26.7 percent. Why was there such a dramatic increase? "What happens is people go across borders and buy guns and bring them into our state," explained Boston Mayor Tom Menino in 2013. "Guns have no borders."[87]

Today, gun enthusiasts love to tout the notion that the city of Chicago has some of the toughest gun laws in the entire country yet ranks among the top for violent, gun-related crimes. To the dismay of these enthusiasts, that myth may have been true a decade ago. "It was indeed a title the city wore proudly," writes Dahleen Glanton of the *Chicago Tribune*:

> We were the only major city that still had an ordinance banning residents from keeping a handgun in their home. The handgun ban made us the primary target of the National Rifle Association and the Second Amendment Foundation, and in 2010 the U.S. Supreme Court forced Chicago to fall into line with the rest of the country. And since then, the courts have peeled off so many layers of our once stellar gun ordinance

that it's barely recognizable. We're still maneuvering to keep gun stores and shooting ranges from opening in the city limits. But the courts have ruled against us on that, too, so we know it's just a matter of time. [88]

That said, the city's ban on assault weapons is still in place, helping to boost Illinois up the ranks to 8th for the toughest gun laws in the country, according to the Giffords Law Center. The state also earns its ranking for a series of laws including tight background checks on gun sales, gun licensing and longer waiting periods between the purchase and transfer of guns.[89]

So why is the gun violence rate so high in Chicago, especially when there are no gun stores in the city and no background check loopholes for private sales? It is near the border of two states, Wisconsin and Indiana, which have different sets of gun laws.

A 2015 study from the University of Chicago demonstrated how permeable borders contribute to gun violence in the Windy City.[90] Researchers were able to trace all new guns recovered from crimes between 2009 and 2013. Their findings showed that 60 percent of these guns used in gang-related crimes were purchased out of state. Of non-gang-related crimes, 32 percent were purchased in other states. Still, many others remained untraceable.

With many states now approving new gun control packages that raises the age on the purchase of all firearms, bans the purchase and possession of bump stocks and sets a longer waiting period to buy any gun, are we really moving in the right direction? Or are gun laws flawed by their very nature?

While their intentions are good and seem promising to mainstream America, these gun control measures are flawed from the start. They are either being implemented via executive order by governors who know very little about guns or rammed through state legislatures so fast that one fatal flaw is overlooked. One need not look any farther than Boston or Chicago — guns don't have borders, and such laws become useless when each state, whose jurisdictions are just as permeable, has their own set of laws.

So, let's say a comprehensive national gun reform bill is passed by Washington and signed into law by the president tomorrow. There is still the issue of our nation's borders being just as porous as any state's or city's. But that shouldn't be a concern considering Mexico has very strict gun laws. According to CBS News, Mexico requires that applicants submit six pieces of documentation: A birth certificate, a letter confirming employment, proof of a clean criminal record from the attorney general's office in the applicant's home state, a utility bill with current address, a copy of a government-issued ID and a federal social security number.[91]

Additionally, the University of Sydney's GunPolicy.org reports that the purchaser must prove a bona fide reason for getting a firearm.[92] In this way, Mexico is like California or New Jersey, but the requirements are at a federal level. Firearms owned by Mexican citizens must then be registered with proper authorities. Moreover, the options for gun purchases are limited to government-approved weapons, which include upwards of 27 brands, from the American Colt, Austria's Glock (used by Seung-Hui Cho at Virginia Tech and Austin Rollins at Great Mills High School) and Italy's Beretta to the locally made Mendoza and Trejo.

Although Mexico has some of the strictest gun laws in the world, the country has a homicide rate more than five times higher than in the U.S., according to CBS News. Arms sales spiked after 2006, when then-President Felipe Calderon took office and declared war on Mexico's drug cartels, who still seem to have no trouble obtaining firearms through international enterprises. These criminal organizations then use them to control territory, extort business owners and threaten citizens as well as members of the security forces.

GUN CONTROL, SCHOOL SAFETY AND THE WAR ON DRUGS

In our earnestness to pass strict gun legislation as a reaction to Parkland, we are overlooking yet another fatal flaw in our logic. Maybe heavy metal vocalist Eric Johns was on to something when he said, "Perhaps the reasons for such tragedies are right under all our noses and we just don't want to see it." Mexico's war on drugs, while well-intended, turned out to be an international failure of epic proportions. In 2002, there were more than 2,600 murder investigations involving firearms.[93] By 2016, that number had increased to nearly 13,000.[94] The country recorded more than 164,000 killings between 2007 and 2014, according to official statistics.

Despite the policies set forth by Attorney General Jeff Sessions, maybe *our* war on drugs is a failure too. If Mexico's statistics aren't eye-opening, maybe *our own* past will be.

The homicide rate in the United States steadily climbed between 1920 and 1933, and the rise of "victimless crimes" — consumption or possession of alcohol — added to the already overburdened judicial system.[95] In addition, alcohol consumption — what prohibition laws sought to minimize — actually increased nearly 70 percent.[96]

According to the Foundation for Economic Education, repealing prohibition destroyed the monopoly on alcohol maintained by organized crime.[97] Disempowering the black market nearly dismantled many enterprises and produced a noticeable decline in the homicide rate, which decreased each year for eleven years straight.[98]

On the comparison between prohibition of the 1920's and gun violence today, FEE writer Jay Stooksberry attempts to put things into perspective:

> There is no doubt that gun violence is a problem. Guns are used in nearly three-fourths of all American homicides.[99] If concerned citizens want to get serious about reducing gun violence, then they should be encouraged to focus less on policies that are ineffective and focus more on ending our failed, four-decade long, overly-militarized, trillion-dollar battle against narcotics.
>
> Why take this approach? Without legal mechanisms in place, the only option for arbitration in the black market is violence. This violence takes many forms: turf wars between drug suppliers where civilians are also caught in the crossfire; no-knock police raids where suspects are gunned down; drug addicts assaulting others to secure money for their addiction. The cycle only gets worse with fathers getting arrested with hefty sentences for victimless crimes such as possession of trace amounts of drugs even without the intent to sell. Their children, sons especially, are then caught up and charged with victimless, non-violent crimes.

According to Mass Shooting Tracker, in 2014, mass shooting incidents resulted in the deaths of 383 people—about 3 percent of total gun homicides for the year.[100] In comparison, the violence caused by the drug war overshadows that of mass shootings. Though difficult to quantify due to inconsistent reporting, estimates of drug-related homicides reach as high as 50 percent of the total homicides in the United States.[101] What does this have to do with Parkland? More than one would think.

When President Richard Nixon declared drug use to be "public enemy No. 1," the number of deaths from the flu (3,707) was nearly doubled the number of deaths involving legal and illegal drugs combined (1,899).[102] Decades after his presidency, Nixon's policies continue to wreak havoc on our nation's youths and minorities. In many cases, catchy slogans like "Drugs are bad" or "Drugs aren't cool" have only increased the allure of illegal substances to adolescents who are eager to test boundaries, find a sense of belonging within gangs who thrive on them or even both.

The "school-to-prison pipeline"[103] is a direct descendant of Nixon's Comprehensive Drug Abuse Prevention and Control Act of 1970, which has been reauthorized under different names by Ronald Reagan and Bill Clinton.[104] This effectively diverted educator attention away from teaching and learning toward scrutinizing student behavior and incentivized over-disciplining students. The pipeline came to represent a disturbing trend in which punitive policies have led to children being funneled out of schools and into the criminal justice system at an alarming rate.

Broward County Public Schools in Florida, the sixth-largest school system in the country, was among the first to embrace programs designed to curb the pipeline, which worsened over time as drugs were funneled up the Florida coast from criminal enterprises in Miami. And Superintendent Robert Runcie played a lead role in implementing new practices designed to handle student behavior issues without resorting to law enforcement involvement, with the goal of ending zero-tolerance policies in schools. But this was an overreaction with little regard for unintended consequences.

"At some point we have to acknowledge that the sheer pain of a Nikolas Cruz or an Adam Lanza, or the children being recruited into gangs is worth addressing," wrote Jodi Jacobson of *Rewire*.[105] "And if we can't completely reorient our thinking on the lost people in this country, we are the only ones to blame for the consequences."

Instead of curbing the pipeline, Runcie overlooked its roots and failed to curb the source. What should have been assessed on a case-by-case basis to correct one's behavior was instead replaced by a systematic "one-size-fits-all" approach. Though Nikolas Cruz did not have any direct ties to gangs, he was able to fall under the radar of local and federal law enforcement thanks to policies set forth by the drug war.

WHAT ABOUT MENTAL HEALTH?

While focusing our efforts on methods to scale down the drug war (or at least its unintended consequences) may seem foreign to some, maybe shifting our focus toward mental health issues is more realistic. A lot has been said about addressing mental health as part of the response to school shootings, and most of it is in the context of preventing someone with a mental illness from obtaining a gun. CNN reported that, according to a 2016 Florida Department of Children and Families finding, Nikolas Cruz "struggled with depression, attention-deficit hyperactivity disorder and autism."[106]

Governor Rick Scott called for $500 million following the Parkland attack, according to NPR.[107] A portion of that funding would give young people more counseling and crisis management. "Florida is never going to be the same — and we've got to make sure Florida is never the same," Scott said. "We've got to make sure we have common-sense solutions to make sure every parent knows that their child is safe."

The mental health provision is attached to a recent controversial gun legislation passed by the Florida Senate.[108] It raises the age of most firearm purchases to 21, institutes a mandatory three-day waiting period for all firearm purchases and bans the sale of bump stocks, devices that can be attached to a weapon to enable it to fire more quickly.[109]

In today's dollars, Florida is spending 40 percent less on mental health than it did in 2000. Melanie Brown-Woofter, president of the Florida Council for Community Mental Health, elaborated, "That means there are fewer providers or sources that the individuals can access. And that lack of resources undercuts the ability to catch mental illness early and treat it. We are really pleased to see the attention and the awareness of mental health services now in the budget," adding that survivors of the shooting may also need ongoing treatment. "More counselors in schools could help students and parents get through situations like this — including families and schools that weren't directly affected."

Both President Trump and Speaker Paul Ryan (R-WI) have pointed to mental health reforms as a solution to school shootings.

"We are committed to working with state and local leaders to help secure our schools, and tackle the difficult issue of mental health," the president said in his first public speech following the attack.[110] But Democrats accused the GOP of misdirecting the national conversation, arguing that the focus must be on gun control over mental health.

"We should fix our mental health system, but we can't let the gun lobby get away with suggesting that mental health is the problem," Senator Chris Murphy (D-CT) said in a statement before claiming that the United States has the highest rate of gun deaths in the world, "The U.S. has the highest rates of gun deaths – not because Americans have higher rates of mental illness than the rest of the world, but because it's so easy for people to get their hands on deadly weapons."

But what about the 2016 *Telegraph* report showing the United States doesn't even crack the top 10 countries in firearm-related deaths? And, what about the role of mental illness in those deaths? Sadly, the one connection between the gunmen involved in the deadly school shootings, the 2009 attack at Fort Hood, Texas, the 2012 movie theater shooting in Aurora, Colorado and the Las Vegas shooting in 2017 is that they had all been in 'psychiatric treatment' prior to the violence.[111]

A review of scientific data published in *Ethical Human Psychology and Psychiatry* regarding the "astonishing rate" of mental illness over the past 50 years revealed that it's not "mental illness" causing the problem, but, rather, the psychiatric drugs prescribed to treat it.[112] In the 1970s, 150,000 American children were taking stimulants for Attention Deficit Hyperactivity Disorder, or ADHD. By 2014, that number had skyrocketed to 4.3 million, an increase of 2,766 percent.

Between 2002 and 2009, pediatric prescriptions for newer antipsychotics increased by 65 percent, from 2.9 million to roughly 4.8 million. "ADHD" and "disruptive behavior" accounted for over 33 percent of all antipsychotic use in children and teens.[113]

The data also showed that mass shootings were occurring more frequently, beginning in 2011. The annual number of mass shootings tripled from an average of five per year between 2000 and 2009 to approximately 15 per year since, according to a 2013 U.S. Justice report.[114] Researchers wanted to know why these attacks were occurring more often and sifted through data from the Food and Drug Administration and found 31 drugs associated with violence.[115]

These drugs, accounting for 79 percent of all the violence cases reported, included 25 psychotropic drugs and included 11 antidepressants, six sedative/hypnotics and three drugs for treatment of ADHD. In the report, the top violent cases included homicide, physical assaults, physical abuse and homicidal ideation.

Withdrawal from psychotropic drugs has also been linked to violent or aggressive behavior, according to a study published in *Psychotherapy and Psychosomatics*. Some of the symptoms may last "several months to years" and include disturbed mood, persistent insomnia, emotional lability, irritability, depression, impaired concentration and memory and poor stress tolerance.

The question begging to be asked is how do we go about limiting access to guns for the mentally ill? While certain mental health background checks at points of purchase have been found to violate HIPAA laws, there were approximately 5.2 million mental health records in the system as of January 2018, a staggering increase from only 234,628 in 2005.

Red flag policies, or extreme risk protection orders, that focus not on dangerous behavior over mental health diagnoses, are beginning to be adopted nationwide. At least 20 states and the District of Columbia have considered such legislation this year, joining Rhode Island, who just passed the policy, and Connecticut, California, Washington and Oregon, who have already seen evidence of suicide prevention.[116]

"To claim, 'Oh, well, you should see the signs and tell law enforcement,' to me is disingenuous unless there is something law enforcement can do," said Avery Gardiner, the co-president of the Brady Campaign to Prevent Gun Violence. Red flag laws, she said, "provide a path to remove guns from somebody in a temporary crisis." Even if a family decides not to seek a gun restraining order, the fact that the option exists can prompt open and honest conversations with struggling relatives.

In some areas, red flag laws remain a topic of controversy due to differing interpretations of what "dangerous behavior" actually means and who is deeming that individual to be "dangerous." Tim Polk had his gun confiscated and told WLNS, Lansing, Michigan's ABC affiliate, "If somebody don't like you, they can say that, and if somebody has something against you (your gun can be taken away)."[117]

The official statement by the American Civil Liberties Union states, "To be constitutional, red flag policies must at a minimum have clear, nondiscriminatory criteria for defining persons as dangerous and a fair process for those affected to object and be heard by a court."[118]

Although gun owners go through due process when their mental health is in question, it is ultimately up to a judge to determine one's stability and not a jury or physician. Rhode Island's newly-passed legislation has been the target of its local ACLU chapter, stating that the court order authorized by the legislation "could be issued without any indication that the person poses an imminent threat to others." Furthermore, no evidence is needed that he or she has ever committed or threatened to commit violence with a firearm. The court's decision would also be made at a hearing where the person would not be entitled to council.[119] Among other points raised by the Rhode Island ACLU:

- The standard for seeking and issuing an order is so broad it could routinely be used against people who engage in "overblown political rhetoric" on social media or against alleged gang members when police want to find a shortcut to seize lawfully-owned weapons from them.
- Even before a court hearing is held, and a decision is made, on a petition for an ERPO, police could be required to warn potentially hundreds of people that the individual might pose a significant danger to them.

- Without the presence of counsel, individuals who have no intent to commit violent crimes could nonetheless unwittingly incriminate themselves for lesser offenses.

Pro-gun Michigan Senator Mike Green has become concerned about judging someone to be mentally ill when they may not be and told WLNS, "I don't think anybody wants people who are mentally ill to have a gun, but that's a mental health problem. How do you define it? And, who is defining it?"

Senator Steve Bieda (D-MI) supports the red flag bill, even though some might be wrongly accused. "I'd much rather have someone go through a little inconvenience rather than end up with a school that's shot at."

Attorney General Jeff Sessions said he wanted the Justice Department to study how mental illness and gun violence intersect, as it would help law enforcement better understand how they can use existing laws to intervene before school shootings happen.

"It cannot be denied that something dangerous and unhealthy is happening in our country," Sessions told a group of sheriffs in Washington. "In every one of these cases, we've had advance indications and perhaps we haven't been effective enough in intervening."

Department of Health and Human Services Secretary Alex M. Azar II added that the administration would be "laser-focused on getting Americans with mental illness the help they need."

"Good school security is a people issue as much as it is a product/hardware issues," said Ken Trump, the president of the National School Safety and Security Services. "The number one way we find out about a weapon or a plot is when kids come forward and tell an adult they trust, not through a metal detector. We need to make sure we have a greater focus on mental detectors, not metal detectors, and we're looking at mental health needs."[120]

While it's true that there are less school shootings today than during the 1990's, there has clearly been a recent uptick in such events. Why is this? Has something changed in our schools over the past couple of years? It might be worth looking into whether they are helping children achieve true success or hindering the kind of development and learning that comes naturally to a child.

Ryan Petty has called for comprehensive change and voiced support for measures such as improving school security and expanding mental health awareness after his daughter, Alaina, was killed in the Parkland attack. He urged people to "walk up, not out" during the National School Walkout on March 14th. His calls on Twitter, along with others' nationwide, prompted the #WalkUpNotOut movement as a means of combating bullying. Petty tweeted a screenshot from Maryland blogger Kelly Guest that said:

> Instead of walking out of school in March 14, encourage students to walk up. Walk up to the kid who sits alone at lunch and invite him to sit with your group; walk up to the kid who sits quietly in the corner of the room and sit next to her. ... Walk up to your teachers and thank them; walk up to someone who has different views than you and get to know them -- you may be surprised at how much you have in common.

Another one of Petty's tweets read, "If you really want to stop the next shooter, #WalkUpNotOut."[121]

Can this approach really play a key role in possibly stopping the next school shooting from occurring? Nobody knows for sure. Isabelle Robinson, a student at Marjory Stoneman Douglas High, miraculously survived the shooting and recalled a few incidents she had with Cruz in a *New York Times* editorial titled, "I Tried to Befriend Nikolas Cruz. He Still Killed My Friends."

Her first interaction occurred during lunchtime when she was in seventh-grade, when Cruz threw an apple at her:

> I felt a sudden pain in my lower back. The force of the blow knocked the wind out of my 90-pound body; tears stung my eyes. I turned around and saw him, smirking. I had never seen this boy before, but I would never forget his face. His eyes were lit up with a sick, twisted joy as he watched me cry. I don't remember if Mr. Cruz was confronted over his actions, but in my 12-year-old naïveté, I trusted that the adults around me would take care of the situation.

She continued with further experiences:

> A year after I was assaulted by Mr. Cruz, I was assigned to tutor him through my school's peer counseling program...Despite my discomfort, I sat down with him, alone. I was forced to endure his cursing me out and ogling my chest until the hourlong session ended. When I was done, I felt a surge of pride for having organized his binder and helped him with his homework.

> Looking back, I am horrified. I now understand that I was left, unassisted, with a student who had a known history of rage and brutality.

Robinson concluded by stating:

> It is not the obligation of children to befriend classmates who have demonstrated aggressive, unpredictable or violent tendencies. It is the responsibility of the school administration and guidance department to seek out those students and get

them the help that they need, even if it is extremely specialized attention that cannot be provided at the same institution.[122]

This is where our new policies have fallen short and is exactly why bullying has grown as a problem in recent years. It is not that children are unequipped to deal with bullies. It is that school discipline policies that discouraged bullying have been replaced by those that urged schools to limit repercussions (with the overall goal of addressing the disproportionate rate of suspensions between white students and their minority counterparts). Under the change, which states adopted and pushed down to counties and municipalities, teachers and other school officials have lost the ability to discipline when warranted.

Although the strategy has seen its share of success stories, it has also allowed countless others to fall through the cracks.

For instance, Nicole and Josh Landers had three children in the Baltimore County public school system in Maryland. All three claimed to have faced threats of bullying and even sexual harassment and said very little, if anything, has been done to address it, even with parental involvement in the house and with school administrators.

One morning, Nicole woke to find her 9-year-old son, Jared, holding a note, which read, "Kill me. I mean nothing. I have issues," since his repeated attempts to report physical harassment and bullying incidents to school officials led nowhere.

Their daughter, Tamar, recalled, "I was sexually harassed by a student, and he would constantly come and touch me and thrust his hips (at me)." Still, nothing was done after speaking with teachers and administrators.

Their son, Justin, a high school senior in the district, told a teacher about a student who brought a knife to school. "The student was gone for a while, but when he came back, he threatened my son," Josh told *Underreported.* "We asked that he be removed from the bus and were told, 'He has rights' and if Josh felt threatened then he can find another way to school."

"What's distressing to us, said Nicole, "is as we've gone through the process, we've had police tell us to stop using the administration and tell our children to go outside of the school and activate 911 instead of getting help from the school."

Josh then added, "We went from a policy that had zero tolerance, to extreme tolerance. That has caused chaos in the classrooms and disarmed teachers to control their classes and stay safe and protected."

Ann Miller, a member of the board with Baltimore County Public Schools, offered her take:

> At first, I thought this was an issue in that school, or that it was isolated. But the more I was hearing very similar stories, the more I realized it's not just a local issue – it's nationwide....My hands are tied due to the layers of state and federal regulations. But if you don't discipline or mischaracterize it, that is as harmful as any potential discriminatory discipline.[123]

Play is critical to the healthy growth and development of children, especially those with learning disabilities such as Cruz. As children play, they figure out how to solve problems, get along with others and develop the fine and gross motor skills needed to grow and learn. It can even be used as a form of therapy to children. Yet many educators are negating the benefits of play by limiting it, often dramatically, and even going so far as banning "best friends." Even worse, several pre-schools have opted to go that route.

Some school officials feel that kids become "more well-adjusted when they have larger friend groups and can avoid negative feelings associated with feeling left out." But some parents argue this "robs children of the chance to form valuable coping skills. By grappling with mild social exclusion when they're young, kids will emerge as more capable, resilient adults." [124]

While this may be up for debate, many studies, including one published in *Child Development*, concluded that those with best friends growing up had better overall mental health into adulthood. Conversely, those with broader friend groups tended to grow up with higher rates of social anxiety than kids with smaller numbers of closer friends. [125]

Aside from limiting discipline or even a child's natural inclination to connect with others, play time has been cut in an effort to focus on academics. This in and of itself has its major pitfalls thanks to programs like No Child Left Behind and Common Core, which take a standardized one-size-fits-all approach to education instead of giving teachers the freedom to cater to the needs of individuals, groups or demographics.

Students with learning disabilities, no matter how major, can easily fall through the cracks. Sudden outbursts by those with special needs may even be misdiagnosed as having ADHD when in fact faculty and administrators, who are already overburdened, lack the training or resources needed to handle some who have been mainstreamed. Communities that don't strictly adhere to the program's guidelines risk funding cuts, and teachers their careers.

Teacher-blogger Jose Vilson summed up his perspective in a 2014 *US News* article, "People who advocate for these standards miss the bigger picture. They came as a package deal with the new teacher evaluations, higher stakes testing, and austerity measures, including school closings in communities who need them most."

Though Common Core allows students to be benchmarked against each other across the country and even globally, its incentive-based model has proven to be inappropriately applied to education. So far, the results have shown an over-reliance on standardized testing used to rate students, teachers and schools, leading to stressed out students, frustrated teachers, anxious administrators and parents scratching their heads over the curricula and how to help their own children.[126] And since the program's incentives come in the form of federal funding for local school departments, municipalities have frowned on giving parents the choice of opting their children out of such programs or exams, even calling it a "dangerous" request.[127]

Would any one of these recently-enacted policies help push an already anxious child over the edge? They should be worth looking into since many states now want to enact mental health initiatives.

What if we can target the source of various key mental health issues rather than treating the symptoms after the fact? One Texas school claims they beat ADHD simply by tripling recess time.[128] Instead of 20 minutes of recess per day, kindergarteners and 1st graders at Eagle Mountain Elementary in Fort Worth now get an hour, broken up into four 15-minute breaks, in addition to lunch.

According to Donna McBride, a 1st grade teacher at the school, the students are "less fidgety and more focused. They listen more attentively, follow directions and try to solve problems on their own instead of coming to the teacher to fix everything. There are fewer discipline issues."[129]

The difference is also in the pencils, claims Cathy Wells, who also teaches 1st grade, "You know why I was sharpening them? Because they were grinding on them, breaking them and chewing on them. Now, they're actually using their pencils for the way that they were designed – to write things!"

Eagle Mountain is one of only a handful of schools in Texas, Oklahoma and California testing out extra recess time as part of a three-year trial. The pilot program, Let's Inspire Innovation 'N Kids, was created by Texas Christian University kinesiology professor Debbie Rhea and is modeled after the Finnish school system, where students have continuously excelled at reading, math and science – and always go outside, even if it's drizzly or cold.

"You start putting 15 minutes of what I call reboot into these kids every so often and... it gives the platform for them to be able to function at their best level," Rhea said.

LiiNK's website says benefits of frequent recess include increased attentional focus, as well as improved academics, attendance, creativity and social skill development. Moreover, recess has been proven to decrease behavioral diagnoses like anxiety, ADHD and anger.[130] The program aims to assess each student differently and advocates for less standardized testing. Still, it is too early to tell how LiiNK or other programs like it will affect students in the United States as they enter middle and high school since every child has different needs and unique experiences as they grow. And, as with any other issue, what is learned in school isn't always carried through at home.

A BREAKDOWN OF THE AMERICAN FAMILY & A DISCONNECTION FROM THE REAL WORLD

In our efforts to do what is right following the Parkland shooting, are we overlooking something more serious and pressing? The one thing that seems to be missing from the conversation today is the lack of emotional support provided to boys, specifically during the time of adolescence. Even more elusive is the question of why more support is needed in the first place. A 2015 investigation found that since Columbine in 1999, the "more than 40 people charged with similar-style plots" were mostly white male teenagers.[131] Why is this?

A CNN story concluded that adolescent boys have a higher risk for lowered impulse control, which makes them more likely than girls to execute a violent crime.[132] Additionally, boys are more likely than girls to blame others for their problems, resulting in the development of anger and hostility.[133] A 2013 study of college students showed that while women saw stalking as harmful, men tended to blame the victims.[134] Research on bullying has also found that boys are more likely than girls to become a bully.[135] And those boys who are the subject of such bullying generally don't ask for help in these situations.

Wes Lammers, then a junior at Columbine, told reporters, "The jocks would make fun of these guys (Eric Harris and Dylan Klebold) and tease them."

Brooks Brown, then a senior who was on "bad terms" with Harris, had miraculously survived the shooting, even though the two came face to face during the melee and later recalled, "He had told me he was going to kill me and had threatened my friends. But, on that day, I had bumped into Harris. All he said was, 'I like you now, go home.'"

Bree Pasquale, another survivor, told the *Denver Post*, "He (Klebold) put a gun to my face and said, 'I'm doing this because people made fun of me last year.'"[136]

This pattern has only repeated itself with just about every mass shooting, from Adam Lanza at Sandy Hook to Dylan Roof's 2016 church shooting in Charleston, South Carolina to Nikolas Cruz. However, bullying is not the only cause for violence.[137]

Sharon Begley, a writer for *Newsweek,* argued in a 1999 article titled "Why the Young Kill" that nature and nurture account for biological roots.[138] "Early experiences seem to be most powerful to a child.

It has been said that spirituality is to religion as romance is to marriage.[139] While that may be a loaded statement, what is true is that marriages do begin to crumble once the initial romance disappears. Can the same be said of the world around us?

A growing number of young people now live in a world without any real meaning. They feel there is nothing for them to believe in and are left emotionally numb. They no longer value themselves for their inherent worth and dignity and find little value in their beliefs.

Instead, many of our young people look elsewhere for validation, such as material goods and social feedback, which ultimately leave many feeling superficial or unfulfilled.

Several global studies seem to suggest that children raised with religion – any (unadulterated) religion – are psychologically healthier than kids raised without it.[140] And teachers have reported that children who attend religious services have stronger self-control and react better to discipline.[141] One reason could be that religious networks provide social support to parents, which can improve their parenting skills. Children who are brought into these networks and hear parental messages reinforced by other adults may also "take more to heart the messages that they get in the home," as long as they are productive rather than forceful in nature.

According to Dr. Michael Ungar, Ph.D., author of *Nurturing Resilience* and contributor to *Psychology Today*, when a child, family or community are facing major events like a natural disaster, violence or unemployment, or even just everyday stressors, a religious community can "provide resources that are difficult to find elsewhere." These resources can include relationships, a sense of identity, power and control, advocacy, rituals and culture and a general sense of belonging.[142] The kids whose parents regularly attended religious services – especially when both parents frequently did – and talked with their kids about religion were rated by both parents and teachers as having better self-control, social skills and approaches to learning than kids with non-religious parents. Even the most hardened criminals have at one point turned to religion through a show of remorse for their actions, praying they don't get caught or even during the loss of someone close. Conversely, children were more likely to have problems when parents confuse teaching with preaching or argue frequently about religion, creating a source of tension in the family.

As the country becomes more secular in nature, children who don't participate in any religious activities can do just as well. The important thing is that they find similar forms of support, are instilled with a keen sense of moral values or channel potentially negative energy through positive outlets like sports, writing or various social clubs. However, the overextension of oneself can have the opposite effect by inadvertently adding stress through lack of time and decreased focus.

Spirituality can also help children cope with many stressors by offering a sense of connection to a world larger than themselves. In a 2015 *Psychology Today* article, Dr. Josh Gressel, Ph.D. reasoned that nature is one of the easiest ways to feel grounded by offering the most direct paths to introspection, including a hike in the woods, time at the beach, a mountain vista or even just gazing up at the stars at night:

> These experiences simultaneously connect us to our deeper selves and to our relative smallness in the grandeur of life. Our ego is temporarily suspended, and we feel ourselves as the souls we are. Even if this connection does not happen in nature, I think it happens when we connect to the spirit that animates a particular thing, be it a baby's smile, the artistry of a piece of jewelry or music.

According to Pacific Standard, research has found "significantly higher levels of anxiety and depression among listeners of heavy metal and hard rock music compared with non-listeners."[143] Because of this stigma, "metalheads" have often been labeled "outcasts" for not following social trends. However, many global studies have sought to understand why heavy metal has a higher percentage of depression among its listeners than other genres, and each conclusion echoes the next – it "combats emotions like depression and anger."[144]

"When I'm sad I don't want to listen to 'Happy' by Pharrell. I want to listen to something that matches my emotions," stated Leah Sharman from the University of Queensland's School of Psychology. "It's about connecting to the music that way."

Jarren Craiig Taylor, vocalist and lyricist for the band Sanguinary Mechanicalism – Nonpsyche, further explained:

> The art (of metal) is typically quite profound. But most importantly it made me realize that humanity is inadvertently dark and violent, but I felt more real and aware listening to it because I outwardly embraced that dark side as opposed to suppressing it until it became something worse.

Regardless of what genre of music one may prefer, there is a pride in having composed music and/or written lyrics that are real and powerful. And even just listening to music composed in such a way can offer a grounded sense of purpose and meaning.

Begley noted in her *Newsweek* article the dark side of nature and nurture is that the young brain is extra-vulnerable to hurt, such as abuse, neglect, terror or family strife, in the first few years of life, and physical changes may occur in the brain if these happen."

Nowhere has this been more evident than during a divorce, which to a child or adolescent can be traumatic. Though exact causes and situations may differ, such as finances, lack of communication, addiction, infidelity, verbal abuse and domestic violence, it can leave lasting effects on impressionable children and adolescents. Many families have even been ripped apart through legal issues or trouble with the law.

"If parental care is inadequate, unsupportive or has broken down," according to Michael Meaney, a biologist at McGill University, "the brain may decide that the world 'stinks,' and just want to disconnect.

The child might even stop caring about themselves or the people around them."

Dr. Warren Farrell, author of the book *The Boy Crisis*,[145] explained:

> The rate of mass shootings has tripled since 2011. We blame guns, violence in the media, violence in video games and poor family values. Each is a plausible player. But our daughters live in the same homes, with the same access to the same guns, video games, and media, and are raised with the same family values. Our daughters are not killing. Our sons are.
>
> But boys with significant father involvement are not doing these shootings. Without dads as role models, boys' testosterone is not well channeled. The boy experiences a sense of purposelessness, a lack of boundary enforcement, rudderlessness, and often withdraws into video games and video porn. At worst, when boys' testosterone is not well-channeled by an involved dad, boys become among the world's most destructive forces. When boys' testosterone is well channeled by an involved dad, boys become among the world's most constructive forces.

Terry Brennan, co-founder of Leading Women for Shared Parenting, notes:

- 72 percent of adolescent murders grew up without fathers, and the same holds true for 60 percent of all rapists.
- 70 percent of juveniles in state institutions grew up in a single-or no-parent situations.
- The number of single-parent households is a much better predictor of violent crime in a community than

looking toward the amount of people living in poverty.[146]

Does this mean that each boy who grows up without a father will become a mass murderer? Of course not. But it does show a disturbing pattern given each mass murderer grew up without a father present.[147] The only exception was Seung-Hui Cho, the Virginia Tech shooter who, like every other shooter, was on psychotropic medication.

Our children's reliance on the internet – social media, online gaming, etc. – is also increasing at a staggering rate. Though this can be seen as a good thing, a key drawback is those who may have accessed the web for educational purposes may begin to use it, along with online gaming, as outlets to vent negative emotions in an attempt to replace them with positive ones.[148] In addition, since the internet is accessible 24-7, they feel more in control in that environment. If they go through a real-life problem, the internet is always there as a source to relieve their stress or to anonymously connect with someone going through the same situations.

While in some respects that may be a good thing, most children actually prefer it over seeking help or talking to someone close to them. Additionally, their over-reliance on the internet as an outlet can lead to over-stimulation, resulting in depression, anxiety, pessimism, difficulty in concentrating, insomnia and irritability from suppressed inner anger. Even worse, this over-stimulation can lead to online addiction with children looking for more ways to find entertainment or fulfillment.

"We are raising a generation of children who know how to tweet and text but don't know how to hold a conversation," stated Fox News contributor Bernard Goldberg back in 2014.[149] Maybe that is the reason why the students of Parkland and their millions of followers have opted to talk down at elected officials rather than speak with them in a productive manner.

This disengagement from reality has become extremely dangerous for several other reasons. Our children are now more comfortable playing dark video games or sharing content over social media with strangers than interacting face to face with someone they know. Some are so attention-starved that they would do anything for likes and shares. But what each of these children need to realize is that information shared is accessible to anyone, and it can easily fall into the wrong hands or culminate with being on either end of constant cyber-bullying.

Moral relativism has also replaced a greater meaning. For instance, the fragility of those known as "snowflakes" shows their emotional vulnerability. Many interpret ideas that challenge their own as acts of aggression. Many resort to harsh or even violent measures to silence disagreeable opponents, leaving little room, if any, for rational discussion.[150]

In the end, our reliance on electronic devices has left us with a disconnection from the real world. What started out as a strong personal relationship with a friend or loved one may have over time become trivialized, resulting in a lack of purpose and self-worth.

Dr. Steve Taylor, Ph.D., who offered this explanation in *Psychology Today*:

> Purpose is a fundamental component of a fulfilling life. It makes us less self-centered, and we feel a part of something bigger. It makes us less vulnerable to external unease and less immersed in thoughts which trigger negative emotions and actions. Human beings crave it and suffer serious psychological difficulties when we don't have it. A lack of

purpose makes us more vulnerable to boredom, anxiety and depression. [151]

CAN WE AVOID SLIPPERY SLOPES?

Given what we know about the previous mass shootings and what led up to them, our focus needs to be honed into tried and true solutions. And for them to work, they need to be implemented by those who are knowledgeable about school safety, firearms or both. Simply taking up a seat in a state legislature with an appealing letter next to one's name will not cut it, nor will heeding the calls of the talking heads on either side of the discussion. Otherwise we stand the risk of falling for measures that sound good in theory, only to create more slippery slopes than they are worth.

Former Education Secretary Arne Duncan and Pam Bosley, co-founder of Purpose Over Pain, a gun control advocacy group, seem to think that gun laws alone will solve everything and have even gone so far as calling for a national school boycott:

> What would happen if millions of parents across America kept their kids out of school for a few days this fall to put pressure on Congress to pass gun safety laws? With the midterm elections coming and control of Congress hanging in the balance, would our politicians finally do something about the mass shootings in schools and other public places? Maybe we should find out.[152]

The two even conceded that the idea seems "counterintuitive" but still think it's acceptable for students to miss some days during the most important part of the school year to make a political point rather than advocate for solutions.

Should we pass laws just for the sake of passing them, regardless of how knowledgeable our elected officials are about firearms? One such instance happened with the April 12th passage of Rhode Island's bump stock ban, which the general assembly hastily put together with very little knowledge about what bump stocks are. A portion of the bill reads:

> It shall be unlawful for any person within this state to modify any semi-automatic weapon such that it can shoot, is designed to shoot, or can be readily restored to shoot full automatic fire with a single pull or hold of the trigger.[153]

The problem with such verbiage is there are no modifications done to the trigger of the weapon. A bump stock is simply a replacement for the butt stock. The trigger is still pulled every time a round is fired. The stock just allows it to happen quicker. Based on the wording of this bill, bump stocks would still be legal because it doesn't change the trigger assembly, and the trigger is still manipulated for each round fired. While other states rush to enact their own sets of laws, it is highly probable that similar mistakes will be made by those with good intentions but have very little knowledge about the firearms they wish to regulate.

One such senator is Diane Feinstein (D-CA), who in 2013 pushed a ban that suffered a basic flaw in that it defined the prohibited guns based on features with little or no functional significance in the context of violent crimes such as barrel shrouds, a covering that protects the shooter's hand from the heat generated by firing a rifle. Additionally, her bill specifically exempted the Iver Johnson M1 carbine and the Ruger Mini-14 rifle, but only when they have fixed stocks. Adding a folding or adjustable stock to these rifles transforms them from legitimate firearms into proscribed "assault weapons," even though that change does not make them any more lethal or suitable for mass murder. A folding stock makes a rifle shorter for transport or storage, while an adjustable stock allows a more comfortable fit for shooters of different sizes.

Sadly, misunderstandings like these are a recurring theme in the subject of gun control. In 2007, Representative Carolyn McCarthy (D-NY) introduced a bill that would have banned semi-automatic rifles with barrel shrouds. She later confessed in an interview with MSNBC that she actually didn't know what a barrel shroud was, "I'm assuming it's a shoulder thing that goes up."[154]

Although "assault weapons" fire no faster than any other semi-automatic, like the Glock 19 pistol or Ruger 10/22 hunting rifle, politicians repeatedly confuse them with machine guns. In fact, Barack Obama and Hillary Clinton often say "machine guns" or "automatic weapons" when they are talking about semi-automatic rifles, perhaps on purpose.

According to a 2013 Reason-Rupe survey, about two-thirds of Americans mistakenly thought "assault weapons" fire faster than other guns, hold more rounds, or use higher-caliber ammunition. The respondents who believed this to be accurate were especially likely to say such guns should be banned. In CBS News polls since 1995, public support for banning "assault weapons" has ranged from 44 percent to 70 percent. Quinnipiac University polls since 2013 have consistently shown most respondents support a nationwide "assault weapon" ban, reaching a high of 67 percent a few days after the Parkland shooting.

Josh Sugarmann, founder and executive director of the Violence Policy Center, devised a strategy of misdirection in a report on "Assault Weapons and Accessories in America." In it, he stated:

> The weapons' menacing looks, coupled with the public's confusion over fully automatic machine guns versus semi-automatic assault weapons – anything that looks like a machine gun is assumed to be a machine gun – can only increase the chance of public support for restrictions on these weapons.

He also argued that because "few people can envision a practical use for these guns, the public should be more inclined to support a ban on 'assault weapons' than a ban on handguns," despite the latter being the most common firearm used in violent crimes.

The faulty logic actually works to benefit those who support "broader gun control" in that once people realize banning these firearms has no measurable effect on violence, they may want to push greater comprehensive measures. Additionally, if the arguments in favor of these bans are enough to survive judicial review, the Second Amendment protections will have been weakened.

There are also those who call for the NRA to get·out of Washington politics. And maybe they should even though the group, along with gun makers and gun rights issues do not even show up on the OpenSecrets website lists for top lobbying firms,[155] top lobbying sectors,[156] top lobbying issues,[157] or top lobbying industries[158] over the last 10 years.

But in all fairness, what about Planned Parenthood or any other centralized lobbying groups that do top Washington's donation lists? Maybe getting them out as well would make our elected officials become more accountable to the very constituents who put them there in the first place. A lot of problems would be solved by bringing

Washington back to a more local level instead of having constituents feel powerless as they watch their elected officials sniff out the money.

In our attempts to take corrective action, we must be careful to avoid slippery slopes. As we act to strengthen mental health checks and requirements, how would that affect HIPAA privacy regulations? While many states are close to passing legislation that raises the minimum age to purchase a weapon from 18 to 21, loopholes *will* be created, only to pose even more questions. Although it is hard to determine whether such an age restriction would actually work, we must remember Rollins was 17, Cho was 23, and Lanza used his mother's rifle.

Then there's the question that if 18-year-olds can enter the armed forces and be entrusted with firearms, would they be excluded from such legislation upon their exit? And, would concerns like PTSD play a role in this decision? Additionally, a gun control advocate might say, "Well, they were taught to take orders in the army and not think for themselves." If that is the case, then it might be valid to wonder, albeit snarkily, if 18-year-olds are mature enough make rational decisions at the polls without bias or voting on impulses based on opinions a teacher may try to pass over as "facts."

Should AR-15 style weapons even be in civilian hands? Maybe we should have thought of that before letting the ban expire in 2004. There are now millions in circulation and counting. Even though there are valid arguments to be made on both sides of this hotly debated topic, would it be right to enact a civil asset forfeiture-style policy and take a commodity from legal owners just because we don't agree with it or like the way it looks? Connecticut just banned the practice, becoming the 14th state to require a criminal conviction for most or all forfeiture cases.[159] Even David Hogg implied in his profanity-laced interview with *The Outline*[160] that he is against it, regardless of whether it falls under such a statute:

> Since our old-ass parents don't know how to use a fucking democracy, we have to. It's alright that people are buying more guns. I just care that they're being safe. They can practice their second amendment rights all they want. I don't give a fuck about that.

Hogg also railed against the legislation Representative Neville has repeatedly proposed, saying:

> It makes me think what sick fuckers are out there that would continue to sell more guns, murder more children and get re-elected. What kind of person are you when you want to see more fucking money than children's lives? What kind of shitty person does that?

When specifically asked about Florida Governor Rick Scott's proposal to bring protective measures such as metal detectors into schools, Hogg brushed it off:

> With Rick Scott, it's like, "When I get elected to senate..." We're not going to let that fucking happen." (Turns and points directly at the camera) And you better not either.[161]

The reality is the legislation he's repeatedly called for goes against his very words. Illinois recently passed HB 1465,[162] which prohibits anyone under 21 years of age from buying or possessing commonly owned semi-automatic rifles, high-capacity weapons that can hold more than 10 rounds, their subsequent attachments, and .50-caliber rifles and cartridges. Those under 21 would have 90 days to turn in their guns to the government or risk becoming criminals.[163] A similar ordinance went into effect in Deerfield, Illinois, where anybody who owns a semi-automatic weapon must turn it in or face a fine of up to $1,000 per day.[164]

Would banning specific weapons like the AR-15 work to keep schools safe? Under the current goals of the hashtag movements, most likely not (though in time, it *might* cut down the number of shootings if we overlooked the millions already in circulation). Knives had been brought into schools like Franklin Regional Senior High School in Murrysville, Pennsylvania and even Stoneman Douglas High School in Parkland, and a bomb that had "great potential to cause significant injury or death" into Pine View High School in St. George, Utah.

A video taken in March at a Rocky Point PTA meeting in Long Island, New York even shows a concerned father making a strong case for protective measures:[165]

> It would probably take the cops 3 to 5 minutes to come here — probably 10 if the traffic's bad. What are you gonna do? (Pauses to take a knife out of his pocket) It's not a gun, but I can do a lot of damage with it. I have two girls in this school. What are you gonna do?

"That's illegal!" yelled one attendee in shock. "He just brought a switchblade into a classroom — he can't do that...is he insane? That's ridiculous and completely illegal!"

"Fearmonger," another called out.

Both Cho and Rollins, the gunmen at Virginia Tech. and Great Mills, respectively, didn't even use rifles — they used pistols that were legal even in highly regulated Mexico, proving yet again that guns don't know state or even international borders.

We have now reached a point where emotions have begun overriding logic in our short-sighted attempts to make a point that unintended consequences have already taken shape. Publix Supermarkets, a Florida-based grocery chain, has been known to make political contributions over the years. However, one in particular caught the attention of David Hogg, who launched a boycott and announced "die-ins" that occurred May 25th at their stores over reports that the company had donated $670,000 in three years to

GOP gubernatorial hopeful Adam Putnam, who also happens to be an unapologetic NRA supporter.

As a result, Publix issued the following statement:

> We would never knowingly disappoint our customers or the communities we serve. As a result, we decided earlier this week to suspend corporate-funded political contributions as we re-evaluate our giving processes.

Initially viewed as a win, it soon became clear that it was anything but, as the supermarket giant also donated more than $760,000 since 2008 to causes like Planned Parenthood and Democratic committees, including at least two dozen candidates for federal office at odds with the NRA.

They include multiple members of the Black Congressional Caucus, former Democratic National Committee chair Debbie Wasserman Schultz, and Sens. Michael Bennet of Colorado, Richard J. Durbin of Illinois, Amy Klobuchar of Minnesota, Patty Murray of Washington, Bill Nelson of Florida, and Ron Wyden of Oregon. The chain also chipped in for presidential candidates Hillary Clinton and Bernie Sanders in 2016, as well as Barack Obama in 2008, according to campaign finance records posted by Open Secrets. [166]

Every action has a consequence, whether intended or otherwise. We must not let ourselves become so clouded by emotion that it becomes counterproductive and even at odds with our overall goals. Yet, contradiction seems to be a recurring theme.

Dick's Sporting Goods[167] and Walmart[168] have announced they'd stop selling assault-style firearms. That is well within their respective rights. However, they have recently come under fire for limiting the sale of their remaining stock to individuals aged 21 and over.[169] That, too, is within their respective rights. Or is it?

We've already been down this road before with wedding cakes, where businesses did not want to cater to specific clientele solely based on ideological differences.[170] So what? Why would anyone want to spend their hard-earned money at a store that for one reason or another doesn't agree with them?[171] Yet the overwhelming majority believes the business is in the wrong despite the Supreme Court's June 4th ruling.[172] Tar that business in feathers if we must and move on to the next who does want the sale.

Pretty simple, yet now we believe a business is in the *right* in wanting to limit sales based on ideologies? We can't have it both ways. Pass laws if we must, but they must not be based on the narrative of the day or else we run the risk of them contradicting each other, creating even more gray areas.

What about the Oakland coffee shop whose owners wouldn't serve police officers for the "safety of their customers"?[173] Hasta Muerte Coffee said they need the support of the actual community to "keep this place safe, not the police." A statement from the coffee shop on February 16th claimed:

> (An officer) entered our shop and was told by one of our worker-owners that 'we have a policy of asking police to leave for the physical and emotional safety of our customers and ourselves.' Since then cop supporters are trying to publicly shame us online with low reviews because this particular police visitor was Latino.

Who is in the right? Or does it even matter? What this incident *does* bring to light is there is *still* a distrust between communities and the very police we entrust to protect them. If a school shooting occurred in a region where such distrust exists, shouldn't we be fearful that responding officers would rather hide behind their cars instead of rushing into the scene?

It was not long ago that hashtag movements were calling for police forces to stand down (thanks in part to militarization tactics enabled and emboldened by the drug war but applied to minor infractions). Yet advocates of strict gun control measures believe it is only the police, security and military personnel who should be allowed to carry.

While utopian in nature, this sentiment plays right into the very definition of the second amendment, which states, "A well-regulated militia, being necessary to the security of a free state, the right of the people to keep and bear arms, shall not be infringed."

"But that is outdated, and the government will never turn on its people," the gun control advocates say. While we do have a checks and balances system within our government, the entire Antifa[174] movement was based on the notion that President Donald Trump and his supporters are fascist.[175] David Frum of *The Atlantic* even went so far as to say "Trump has already set the conditions to build an autocracy in the U.S."[176] Either they support strict gun control or they believe our government has completely fallen into the wrong hands.

WHEN IS ENOUGH, ENOUGH?

On May 18th, we were all glued to the news once again as word got out that there was an active shooter, this time at Santa Fe High School in Santa Fe, Texas, just south of Houston. Like Parkland just a few months prior, 17-year-old Dimitrios Pagourtzis easily entered the school and killed eight students and two teachers. 13 others lay wounded. But that was where the similarities ended.[177]

Pagourtzis was a student athlete who played on the junior varsity football team, and though described as a "quiet kid," he had no criminal history. Valerie Martin, a teacher at the junior high school in Santa Fe, told the *New York Times* she had Pagourtzis in her pre-A.P. language arts class and saw no warning signs. She described him as "bright" and said he participated in the school's competition for a national history contest.[178]

What drove such a promising student to kill classmates and teachers? It was reported that one of the victims, 16-year-old Shana Fisher, had rejected his advances for months. About one week before the shooting, she stood up to him in the middle of class and said she would not go out with him. Shana's mother, Sadie Baze, said she believes the incident embarrassed Pagourtzis to such a point that he targeted her. "One of the shotgun shells was for my daughter," she said.

Shana's father, Timothy Thomas, told the *Daily Mail* that his daughter predicted Pagourtzis was going to harm her:

> He had told her himself he was going to kill her. He was walking around planning this in his head for two weeks. Shana said that if he came into the school with a gun and killed her she would haunt him for the rest of his life. She was really scared.[179]

His social media footprint told a different story and included an image of a T-shirt prominently displaying the words, "Born to kill" on Facebook, along with additional images of a black duster jacket with Nazi, communist, fascist and religious symbols. Also posted was the phrase, "Dangerous Days" just before the attack, along with a pentagram symbol.

Information in journals, on his computer and on cell only confirmed these fears and even mentioned how Pagourtzis wanted to take his own life afterward.

Two armed resource officers arrived at the school's art lab about four minutes after the shooting started and immediately began trading shots with Pagourtzis. They were then joined by sheriff's deputies, who also traded shots with the gunman and tried to convince him to give up during lulls in the gunfire.

The school attempted to follow lockdown procedures by barricading students in their classrooms. But Zack Wofford who was in math class "at least two doors down" from the initial gunfire, told KHOU that his teacher may have made matters worse:

> My sub pulled the fire alarm. He actually ran out of the classroom and pulled the fire alarm, and we barricaded the

door. The goal was to get the rest of the school out, because on the side ... that [the shooting] happened on, there wasn't a lot of kids. There's only like three or four classes on that section, so we knew there was a whole 'nother thousand [students] on the other side, so we knew a fire alarm would get them safe.[180]

For some students inside the school, the fire alarm made them think the emergency wasn't as dire. Branden Auzston, an 11th grader at the school, thought it may have been a fire since they had a drill two weeks prior. "We go outside, and we were told to get in the grass," Auzston said. "Then I see my teacher, and she screamed 'Just run!'"

Though it's unknown if the fire alarm actually saved lives or put more students at risk, Ken Trump told reporters that a lockdown would have been a better way to ensure safety:

> Reports indicate someone at the school pulled the fire alarm – either a student or perhaps a staff member. My takeaway so far based on what we know is that this is a perfect example of why schools need to practice lockdowns, teach students and teachers the importance of lockdown. When you initiate evacuation by a fire drill, you are creating a target rich environment that is perfect for shooters to cause mass fatalities.

Pagourtzis eventually surrendered to police, who took custody of a Remington 870 short-barreled shotgun and a .38-caliber Rossi revolver at the scene. Explosives and Molotov cocktails were also found at the high school, Pagourtzis' home and in a vehicle, further pushing this attack beyond the media narratives.[181]

As expected, the details fell on deaf ears as the calls of increased gun control grew louder. Upon hearing of the shooting, New York Governor Andrew Cuomo (D) tweeted, "DO SOMETHING," to

President Trump, accompanied by a letter to the president and Congress, which read:

> Columbine. Virginia Tech. Sandy Hook. Las Vegas. Orlando. Parkland. And now, Santa Fe.
>
> When is enough enough? How many more innocent people have to die before you act?
>
> You were elected to lead — do something. Your first responsibility is to the people of this country, not the NRA — do something. My heart breaks for the families who have to grieve from this needless violence — DO SOMETHING.[182]

Former Arizona Representative Gabrielle Giffords (D) offered her insight via Twitter:

> I will not stand for this and neither should you. Parents shouldn't have to hug their children in the morning and worry whether they'll see them at the end of the day. We don't have to live in a country where politicians let this happen again and again.[183]

She later added:

> It's time for America to find the courage to take on the powerful and fight for our own safety. We can't wall ourselves off from the threat of gun violence—it doesn't work. Nor can we simply arm ourselves against one another—that makes it more dangerous still.[184]

Upon hearing of the attack, David Hogg tweeted, "Get ready for two weeks of media coverage of politicians acting like they give a shit when in reality they just want to boost their approval ratings before midterms."[185]

While Giffords may have been on-point with her initial reaction, she, just like Cuomo and Hogg, clearly missed the mark by echoing the calls for greater gun control instead of following the details coming out of Santa Fe.

Nobody was able to answer exactly what "do something" actually meant, and the gun control ideas that were being discussed were not even relevant this time around. No law could have prevented this horrific shooting from occurring.

Pagourtzis, a junior at the school, used a sawed-off shotgun and a .38-caliber revolver, both of which would not have been affected by a federal "assault weapons" ban. Bump stocks are also incompatible with such firearms, and it is already illegal on a federal level to possess a sawed-off shotgun (which enables the ammunition to propel faster than if the barrel was complete).[186]

Furthermore, the guns were legally purchased by his father for his own personal use, so background checks and red flag laws, no matter how universal or comprehensive, would not have applied either.[187] And even if he wanted to purchase a firearm on his own, he wouldn't have been able to since he is below the Texas minimum age of 18.

Still, as anti-gun rhetoric filled news stories nationwide, mixed sentiments of those in and around Santa Fe demonstrated why a greater conversation is needed if we want to truly remain results-oriented.

Lieutenant Governor Dan Patrick (R-TX) spoke with conservative talk show host Mark Levin after the shooting and was asked about his take:

> I met with some of the students at the hospital and asked, 'What is your answer?' And, they all said, 'We need to arm our teachers.' In Texas, we allow that, but we leave it to the local school districts to make that decision...There was a substitute teacher in the room next door, an ex-Marine. And one of the

students said that if he was armed, he would have been able to take out the shooter.[188]

Lt. Governor Patrick rationalized that school districts are given the option of arming their teachers (if they so choose to become certified) because there are municipalities that are so remote that it may take authorities up to 20 minutes to arrive on the scene of an active shooter.

Representative Michael McCaul (R-TX) said, "We need to harden these targets, these soft targets with school resource officers."

Governor Greg Abbott (R-TX) proposed holding round-table discussions, saying he wanted to work on laws that will protect Second Amendment rights while making schools safer. And, area residents have even called for arming teachers, redesigning school buildings and promoting safer gun storage at home to keep firearms out of the hands of children and teenagers.

Monica Bracknell, a senior at Santa Fe High School, spoke with Abbott two days after the shooting with a simple message: The violence is not "a political issue."

She further explained to reporters that even though schools need to be safer, restricting the availability of guns is not the way to achieve it:

> People like to say on Facebook, 'Oh, you shouldn't be able to buy a gun.' That kid was 17. He's not able to buy a gun anyway. It's not a gun-law issue. This kid is obviously mentally unstable, and he knew that there were flaws in the school system to get into the rooms.

Tyler Cruz, an 18-year-old senior, said he would support any gun control movement at his school now but is keenly aware his classmates will be divided. "Our community is really pro-gun here," he said. "I'm pro-gun, but I'm not. I get the Second Amendment, but I just believe it's gotten too far with all this happening."[189]

One student, Paige Curry, solemnly told KPRC-TV, "It's been happening everywhere, I've always kind of felt that eventually it would happen here, too."[190]

Another student, Dakota Shrader, told Fox News, "I shouldn't be going through this. It's my school. This is my daily life. I shouldn't have to feel like that."

In a statement posted on Facebook, Houston police chief Art Acevedo wrote that he had "shed tears of sadness, pain and anger" after the shooting, which occurred just 35 miles south of the city:

> I know some have strong feelings about gun rights, but I want you to know I've hit rock bottom and I am not interested in your views as it pertains to this issue. Please do not post anything about 'guns aren't the problem' and 'there's little we can do.'

> The hatred being spewed in our country and the new norms we, so-called people of faith are accepting, is as much to blame for so much of the violence in our once pragmatic nation.

> This isn't a time for prayers, and study and inaction, it's a time for prayers, action and the asking of God's forgiveness for our inaction (especially the elected officials that ran to the cameras today, acted in a solemn manner, called for prayers, and will once again do absolutely nothing).[191]

Like many before him, he stopped short of offering any kind of solution, only implying that "something" needed to be done. Overlooked yet again were the calls for school safety, and the media tried doing what it could to make "gun control" narratives stick in Santa Fe's wake instead.

Two days after the attack, the *New York Times* lamented that anti-gun furor was not likely in Texas as it was in other areas of the country:

> What played out instead was a reminder, as happened after 26 people were killed in a church shooting in Sutherland Springs, Tex., in November, that major gun violence often does not produce a backlash against guns. The differences in how the issue has played out in Texas and Florida illustrate just how hard it can be to establish a consensus on gun issues in America. For gun control advocates, what works in one part of the country does not work in others, even down to the vocabulary used. Some pro-gun Texans question the phrase 'gun violence' and avoid using it, saying it is as arbitrary as talking about knife violence.

The article's authors, Manny Fernandez, Jack Healy and Dave Montgomery, were optimistic at the future of Texas despite pro-gun forces being "firmly" in control:

> Polling shows the state's voters are more split on guns than popular culture might indicate. According to an October poll by the University of Texas and The Texas Tribune, more than half of the registered voters surveyed said gun control laws should be stricter. Only 13 percent said the laws should be less strict than they are now, and 31 percent would prefer to leave current gun laws unchanged.

During the May 22nd edition of *MSNBC Live with Stephanie Ruhle*, reporter Mariana Atencio spoke with a few members of the school's baseball team, including two who were shot. About halfway through the interview, she asked, "You think about Parkland. It happened in February. There's been a national debate about gun safety and gun reform. What do you guys think should be done?

One of the students, Trenton Beazley, simply advised his peers across the country to "be kind to others."

Atencio then asked, "Have you heard what you want to hear from lawmakers, from the governor, from your senators?"

"I haven't heard much," one of the athletes said. "But I've seen stuff about our school. Somebody said that they're going to be donating metal detectors to our school. But I just think just simply locking the doors to anywhere, just locking the doors from outside, having the kids all come in one way, looking for suspicious things, locking the doors to every classroom. That would prevent a lot of things from happening."

Finally, she asked Beazley, "We saw the teens in Parkland really become the voices of the movement for gun reform across the country. Now your voices have become all important. How do you feel about that responsibility on your shoulders right now, Trenton?"

"It's just kind of, you know, what it is," he objectively replied. "It's sad that it happens everywhere but, you know, you just kind of have to go through it."[192]

With so much emphasis being placed on gun control, and more importantly the shooter, instead of precautionary measures that could have been or should be implemented, Jennifer B. Johnston, PhD, of Western New Mexico University, wanted to know if there was a direct correlation between media coverage and the growing rate of mass shootings.

In 2016, she, along with Andrew Joy, BS, also of Western New Mexico University, sought to find out if the relationship is "unidirectional" in nature – do more shootings lead to more coverage? Or is it possible that more coverage leads to more shootings?" They reviewed data on mass shootings collected by media outlets, the FBI and advocacy organizations, as well as articles by leading scholars.

According to Johnston, "The prevalence of these crimes has risen in relation to the mass media coverage of them and the proliferation of social media sites that tend to glorify the shooters and downplay the victims."[193]

She also suggested that the "media cry to cling to 'the public's right to know' covers up a greedier agenda to keep eyeballs glued to screens, since they know that frightening homicides are their No. 1 ratings and advertising boosters." An additional finding was a commonality among mass shooters of wanting to become famous.

While mass shootings peaked in the late 1990s, Johnston and Joy found evidence that the frequency of such events increased in direct correlation with the emergence of 24-hour cable news coverage. Moreover, the rise of the internet happened during the same period. In addition to a shooter's name being repeated over the news, social media now allowed the public to freely share opinions of the news to millions more, enabling that shooter to become a household name.

"If the mass media and social media enthusiasts make a pact to no longer share, reproduce or retweet the names, faces, detailed histories or long-winded statements of killers, we could see a dramatic reduction in mass shootings in one to two years," Johnson concluded.

While this may not be too realistic with the media's perpetual necessity to attract viewers in an ever-growing competitive landscape, we can learn to control what we seek in our constant thirst for information. We have already done it several times.

For instance, a string of events began in 1986 in which United States Postal Service (USPS) employees shot and killed managers, fellow workers, members of the police and even the general public in acts of mass murder, coining the term "going postal." The constant attention given to these employees only encouraged others outside of the USPS to commit similar acts of murder in the workplace.

However, coupled with workplace policy reforms, the number of employees going postal has decreased dramatically thanks in part to calls on the media to stop giving disturbed individuals the attention they seek or the outlet in which to air their grievances.

There was also a rash of celebrity suicides in the mid-1990s that grew to such an extent that health officials began describing it as "a contagious epidemic." Due to constant media coverage, such deaths began to be viewed as acceptable behavior, and once perceived this way, those experiencing depression may have been more likely to commit suicide as a result.[194] Suicides have also enabled average celebrities and musicians to reach immortality or legendary status in the eyes of their fans. Kurt Cobain's suicide in 1994 even prompted the media to call him "Voice for a generation." By 1997, there was a sharp decline in these suicides, just a couple of years after the Centers for Disease Control convened a working group of suicidologists, researchers and the media, and then made recommendations to them, including a reduction of coverage and even a change of how such stories were to be covered when they did occur.

In stark contrast to Cobain's coverage, the 2017 suicides of musicians Chris Cornell and Chester Bennington were more subdued in nature and focused on their states of mind and mental health awareness over hero worship.

Since recent data suggests suicides are very rare among those with chronic depression, can the same be done with how school violence is covered? After all, each attacker had a story to tell and wanted the world to know their names. Pagourtzis allegedly spared the lives of students he liked in hoping they would tell his story since he originally planned to take his own life. Adam Lanza wanted his name forever etched in history for the Sandy Hook shooting. And, Nikolas Cruz wanted to be equally as famous. Time will tell. But, if history serves as any indicator, it's at least a small step in the right direction of addressing this epidemic of school shootings.

Andrew Pollack, who went on to form Americans for CLASS (Children's Lives and School Safety) now refers to his daughter's murderer simply as "18-1958" (his case number), explaining, "The media shouldn't give evil a face or a voice. 18-1958 did this for fame as witnessed in his videos."[195]

A PATH FORWARD

Since we continue to miss the mark thanks in part to identity politics, exactly how do we best move forward from here? The answer may surprise some. It is simply one word — listen. Listen, but not with our mouths. Listen with our ears and open hearts. If gun control measures are to be passed, they cannot be done so in haste because some person on television or at a march said so. There is a danger in heeding the calls of ideologues on either side without first discussing any and all ramifications. We may even end up missing the entire point of what we can do to keep our schools from remaining soft targets.

The most important thing we can and should do is let open and honest dialogue take its course. Listen not to those you may agree with. Rather, listen to those who have differing views. It is only then that we can begin to understand all sides of the argument so we can move forward in a productive manner. *New York Times* contributor Bret Stephens wrote of identity politics:

> It has become the moated castles from which we safeguard our feelings from hurt and our opinions from challenge. It is our "safe space." But it is a safe space of a uniquely pernicious kind — a safe space *from* thought, rather than a safe space *for* thought.

> The primary test of an argument isn't the quality of the thinking but the cultural, racial, or sexual standing of the person making it. As a woman of color I think X. As a gay man I think Y. As a person of privilege I apologize for Z. This is the baroque way Americans often speak these days. It is a way of replacing individual thought — with all the effort that actual thinking requires — with social identification — with all the attitude that attitudinizing requires. [196]

We must acknowledge flaws and inconsistencies in our logic. To find *true* solutions, we must break out of the mold Stephens talks about. Outcomes with unintended consequences will begin to take shape if gun control advocates and gun enthusiasts alike cling to their respective ideologies and act on emotions.

We must not be naive either by believing laws will solve the crises we find ourselves confronting today. Though they may help curb the number of incidents, they will not address the fact that if someone wants to kill, they will always find a way to do it, with or without weapons, and with or without regulations.

Given the sentiments that have been expressed by the media, survivors and the general public in the wake of the Parkland and Santa Fe shootings, along with the silence over Everett, St. George and even the knives at Stoneman Douglas, the burial of the YouTube attack and the refusal to acknowledge the shock at Rocky Point, we know the hashtag movements are not about school safety at all — they are purely about gun control.

Real solutions include compromise. A good starting point would be to stop advertising our schools and other public places as being soft targets. As reassuring as they may sound, designating locations as "gun-free zones" has only put people at risk by attracting those with mental health issues looking to maximize their impact. Moreover, we must ensure procedures are strictly adhered to, such as background checks and communication between state and local agencies, and any policy flaws are shored up. Our government, who we are imploring to take action, hasn't even done that much on a federal level, yet we are perfectly happy overlooking fatal flaws like these in favor of advancing political objectives.

While it may seem controversial to some, Representative Neville is not merely acting on emotion after the latest school shooting. Regardless of whether we believe a measure like his would work, we can't just put band aids on these issues because they give us the warm and fuzzy feeling we want. We can't discount the value armed resource officers could bring when seconds count, especially since at least two school shootings were stopped in the wake of Parkland. Additionally, despite Ken Trump's beliefs, we can't overlook discussions about metal detectors given our elected officials walk through them every day on their way to work. And offering more emotional support would only work if we addressed root causes rather than treating symptoms with band aids after the fact.

Pass some kind of gun control measure if you must. Just remember those calling for new regulations are more protected than our students, and enacting a law for the sake of saying, "We finally did it" should not inspire confidence in the goal of ensuring school safety. That only brings forth a false sense of security.

Moreover, closure should not come in the form of electing politicians or enacting such a law with barely a meaningful conversation. Doing so can potentially place more children in harm's way. Likewise, heeding the calls to vote for anti-NRA candidates may even be counterproductive and cause us to indirectly support the very same policies that allowed Parkland happen in the first place. There is a bigger picture that must be looked at. Closure can only arrive when we overcome our own personal biases and begin asking the right questions, keeping in mind any short- and long-term ramifications that could arise. The true tragedy would be if they were completely avoidable.

Enough is enough already. If there is one silver lining in the wake of Parkland and its other subsequent attacks, may it be that we have finally learned from past failures and do what is right rather than what sounds good in theory. Aren't our children's lives worth more than the scoring of political points in an election year?

NOTES

Failures of Epic Proportions

[1] http://www.nytimes.com/1999/04/25/weekinreview/the-nation-the-stresses-of-youth-the-strains-of-its-music.html

[2] https://www.metal-archives.com/bands/Simple_Aggression/891

[3] https://www.cnn.com/2013/10/31/us/virginia-tech-shootings-fast-facts/index.html

[4] http://voices.washingtonpost.com/rawfisher/2009/02/va_tech_ignored_more_cho_warni.html

What Makes Parkland Different?

[5] https://www.cnn.com/videos/us/2018/02/17/parkland-florida-student-emma-gonzalez-anti-gun-rally-fort-lauderdale-full.cnn

[6] https://www.wsj.com/articles/a-failure-of-law-enforcement-1519408337

[7] https://www.usatoday.com/story/news/2018/02/22/school-shooting-family-took-accused-shooter-told-police-earlier-he-threatened-guns/365182002

[8] https://www.usatoday.com/story/news/nation-now/2018/02/23/florida-school-shooting-sheriff-got-18-calls-cruzs-violence-threats-guns/366165002

[9] http://www.sun-sentinel.com/local/broward/parkland/florida-school-shooting/fl-florida-school-shooting-response-fail-20180223-story.html

[10] http://www.sun-sentinel.com/local/broward/parkland/florida-school-shooting/fl-florida-shooting-sro-20180222-story.html

[11] https://www.cnn.com/videos/us/2018/02/17/parkland-florida-student-emma-gonzalez-anti-gun-rally-fort-lauderdale-full.cnn

12 http://www.independent.co.uk/news/world/americas/us-politics/david-hogg-gun-control-marjory-stoneman-douglas-new-law-parkland-florida-a8230031.html

13 https://www.actionnetwork.org/event_campaigns/enough-national-school-walkout

14 http://www.sun-sentinel.com/local/broward/parkland/florida-school-shooting/fl-florida-school-shooting-nikolas-cruz-warning-signs-20180216-story.html

15 http://abcnews.go.com/Politics/trump-holds-listening-session-students-mass-shootings/story?id=53245367

16 https://www.aol.com/article/news/2018/02/21/im-pissed-dad-whose-daughter-was-shot-9-times-at-florida-high-school-lays-into-the-messed-up-state-of-america-at-trump-listening-session/23367874

17 http://www.newsweek.com/columbine-florida-school-shooting-gun-control-812173

18 http://www.newsweek.com/florida-shootings-guns-schools-students-809551

19 http://www.sun-sentinel.com/local/broward/parkland/florida-school-shooting/fl-florida-school-shooting-district-stonewalling-20180510-story.html

20 https://www.washingtontimes.com/news/2018/may/14/nikolas-cruz-violated-obamas-promise-diversion-pro

Do We Really Need to Fix What Isn't Broken?

21 http://www.courant.com/breaking-news/hc-br-waterbury-high-school-threat-20180220-story.html

22 http://wavy.com/2018/02/23/va-beach-officials-holding-news-conference-on-recent-school-threats

23 http://www.nbc-2.com/story/37880458/student-arrested-for-bringing-gun-to-fort-myers-high-school

24 https://www.seattletimes.com/seattle-news/crime/everett-teen-arrested-after-grandma-finds-journal-detailing-school-shooting-plot-police-say

Is It Really About School Safety?

25 https://www.usatoday.com/story/news/nation/2018/02/27/rhode-island-red-flag-dangerous-gun-owners/376158002

[26] http://www.golocalprov.com/news/10-babies-dead-in-ri-in-26-months-2-new-near-death-little-outrage

[27] http://turnto10.com/i-team/nbc-10-i-team-exclusive-lawmaker-raises-alarm-about-ris-911-system

[28] http://digital.olivesoftware.com/Olive/ODN/ProJo/shared/ShowArticle.aspx?doc=TPJ%2F2018%2F03%2F20&entity=Ar00101&sk=B9819A8B&mode=text

[29] http://wpri.com/2017/02/22/dcyf-previously-investigated-family-of-infant-who-died-in-warwick

[30] https://mobile.nytimes.com/2017/09/24/opinion/dying-art-of-disagreement.html

[31] http://insider.foxnews.com/2016/07/07/anti-gun-prof-who-called-shooting-nras-hq-it-was-joke

[32] https://soundcloud.com/wcrn-ben/mahar-high-school-teacher-ian-bashaw-on-their-school-walkout

[33] http://sacramento.cbslocal.com/2018/03/14/rocklin-teacher-questions-walkout

[34] http://www.kentucky.com/news/nation-world/national/article205235894.html#fmp

[35] http://www.fox32chicago.com/news/local/chicago-students-trash-walmart-during-walkout-over-gun-violence

[36] https://pjmedia.com/trending/student-assaulted-pro-second-amendment-views-suspended-defending

The AR-15: Separating Fact from Fiction

[37] http://www.nytimes.com/2012/12/26/us/legislative-handcuffs-limit-atfs-ability-to-fight-gun-crime.html

[38] https://www.atf.gov/resource-center/docs/undefined/firearms-commerce-united-states-annual-statistical-update-2017/download

[39] https://ucr.fbi.gov/crime-in-the-u.s/2016/crime-in-the-u.s.-2016/tables/expanded-homicide-data-table-4.xls

[40] https://www.feinstein.senate.gov/public/_cache/files/b/5/b531daeb-a954-41f8-a21c-268cceccb4c4/55A639CA20094C1538C8B7FE50B3A94A.penn-study-koper.pdf

[41] http://www.nytimes.com/2012/12/25/business/real-and-virtual-firearms-nurture-marketing-link.html?hpw

42 http://lawcenter.giffords.org/explore-annual-gun-law-scorecard

Hashtags, Exclusions And Narratives

43 https://ijr.com/2018/03/1074285-parkland-shooting-survivor-responds-to-flotus-hate

44 https://www.realclearpolitics.com/video/2018/02/22/fl_school_shooting_survivor_ariana_klein_networks_dont_want_us_to_give_our_real_opinions_want_us_to_further_their_agendas.html

45 https://www.politico.com/newsletters/playbook/2018/03/22/omnibus-vote-government-spending-257842

46 https://www.npr.org/sections/thetwo-way/2014/04/09/300872511/many-students-stabbed-cut-at-pennsylvania-high-school

47 https://www.cnn.com/2014/04/09/justice/pennsylvania-school-stabbing/index.html

48 https://www.washingtontimes.com/news/2018/apr/9/david-hogg-taking-gap-year-college-work-midterm-el

49 http://www.independent.co.uk/news/world/americas/us-politics/david-hogg-gun-control-marjory-stoneman-douglas-new-law-parkland-florida-a8230031.html

50 http://time.com/5176544/david-hogg-boycott-florida

51 https://www.nbcnews.com/news/us-news/teen-drawn-isis-brought-homemade-bomb-utah-school-police-say-n854351

52 https://www.aol.com/article/news/2018/03/20/two-wounded-in-maryland-school-shooting-student-gunman-dies/23390417

53 https://www.cnn.com/2018/03/20/us/great-mills-high-school-shooting/index.html

54 http://www.sun-sentinel.com/local/broward/parkland/florida-school-shooting/fl-florida-school-shooting-students-arrested-20180320-story.html

55 http://lawcenter.giffords.org/minimum-age-to-purchase-possess-in-maryland

56 http://www.chicagotribune.com/news/local/breaking/ct-met-dixon-school-shooting-20180516-story.html

57 http://wgntv.com/2018/05/16/suspect-shot-after-bringing-gun-to-dixon-high-school-officials-say

58 http://insider.foxnews.com/2018/03/24/march-our-lives-stoneman-douglas-survivor-kyle-kashuv-says-david-hogg-inflammatory-gun

59 https://www.local10.com/news/parkland-school-shooting/brother-of-parkland-shooting-victim-says-he-was-shut-out-of-march-for-our-lives

60 https://marchforourlives.com/resources

61 http://adage.com/article/news/march-life-posters/312747

62 http://gaia.adage.com/images/bin/pdf/neveragainhires_SeanMcSherry.pdf

Are Narratives Based on Good Intentions Putting Our Children At Risk?

63 https://www.youtube.com/watch?v=K-4tVcAho74

64 https://www.campusreform.org/?ID=10687

65 https://reason.com/blog/2018/03/24/march-for-our-lives-guns-schools-safety

66 https://www.facebook.com/cj.westfall.1/videos/10204816015436448

67 https://nypost.com/2018/03/11/parents-up-in-arms-after-nypd-removes-cops-from-schools

68 http://turnto10.com/news/local/hundreds-attend-providence-gun-violence-rally-saturday

69 http://www.golocalprov.com/news/raimondo-says-armed-school-resources-officers-should-be-determined-by-commu

70 http://foxbaltimore.com/news/local/arming-sros-baltimore-school-police-remain-unarmed

71 https://maryland.ourcommunitynow.com/news/baltimore-cant-afford-to-heat-schools-but-will-pay-100k-to-bus-students-to-gun-control-rally

72 https://www.realclearpolitics.com/video/2018/03/23/david_hogg_parkland_hs_has_become_a_prison_hundreds_of_racist_police.html

73 https://www.theblaze.com/news/2018/04/02/citing-private-chats-parkland-teacher-says-students-like-david-hogg-dont-speak-for-all-students

74 https://www.safewise.com/blog/do-fake-security-signs-really-work

75 https://crimeresearch.org/2014/09/more-misleading-information-from-bloombergs-everytown-for-gun-safety-on-guns-analysis-of-recent-mass-shootings

76 https://crimeresearch.org/2018/04/waffle-house-continues-company-policy-ban-permitted-concealed-handguns-civilians-restaurants

77 http://www.thewesterlysun.com/News/Westerly/Westerly-School-Committee-meets-on-March-29.html

78 https://law.justia.com/codes/rhode-island/2012/title-12/chapter-12-7/chapter-12-7-21

79 http://gaia.adage.com/images/bin/pdf/March_DianAriAndryian.pdf

80 http://www.pewsocialtrends.org/2013/05/07/gun-homicide-rate-down-49-since-1993-peak-public-unaware

If Gun Control Is So Great, Why Has It Failed?

81 https://www.cdc.gov/nchs/fastats/homicide.htm

82 http://www.telegraph.co.uk/travel/maps-and-graphics/mapped-the-countries-with-the-most-guns

83 https://www.bostonglobe.com/opinion/2013/02/17/the-nation-toughest-gun-control-law-made-massachusetts-less-safe/3845k7xHzkwTrBWy4KpkEM/story.html

84 http://www.goal.org/masslawpages/storageinfo.html

85http://www.capecodonline.com/apps/pbcs.dll/article?AID=/20020820/NEWS01/308209961&template=printart

86 https://www.bostonglobe.com/opinion/2013/02/17/the-nation-toughest-gun-control-law-made-massachusetts-less-safe/3845k7xHzkwTrBWy4KpkEM/story.html

87 http://www.boston.com/news/local/massachusetts/2013/02/04/gun-crimes-increase-massachusetts-despite-tough-gun-laws/XjlDQLZlUDvsf3KS8PqyGK/story-1.html

88 http://www.chicagotribune.com/news/columnists/glanton/ct-met-gun-control-chicago-dahleen-glanton-20171003-story.html

89 https://www.washingtonpost.com/news/fact-checker/wp/2017/10/17/does-a-city-with-the-toughest-gun-laws-end-up-with-worst-gun-violence/?utm_term=.0d1c8aeb275b

90http://home.uchicago.edu/ludwigj/papers/JCrimLC%202015%20Guns%20in%20Chicago.pdf

91 http://www.cbsnews.com/news/mexicans-have-the-right-to-own-guns-but-few-do

92 http://www.gunpolicy.org/firearms/region/mexico

93http://secretariadoejecutivo.gob.mx/docs/pdfs/estadisticas%20del%20fuero%20comun/2002.pdf

Gun Control, School Safety and The War On Drugs

94 http://secretariadoejecutivo.gob.mx/docs/pdfs/estadisticas%20del%20fuero%20comun/Cieisp2016_012017.pdf

95 http://www.cato.org/pubs/pas/pa-157.html

96 http://www.nber.org/papers/w3675

97 https://fee.org/articles/want-to-stop-gun-violence-end-the-war-on-drugs

98 http://www.cato.org/pubs/pas/pa-157.html#48

99 http://www.statista.com/statistics/195331/number-of-murders-in-the-us-by-state

100 http://www.shootingtracker.com

101 http://www.theatlantic.com/business/archive/2012/12/the-single-best-anti-gun-death-policy-ending-the-drug-war/266505

102 https://news.utexas.edu/2016/04/25/school-to-prison-pipeline-caused-by-war-on-drugs-policy

103 https://www.usnews.com/news/education-news/articles/2018-03-06/did-an-obama-era-school-discipline-policy-contribute-to-the-parkland-shooting

104 http://criminal.findlaw.com/criminal-charges/comprehensive-drug-abuse-prevention-and-control-act-of-1970.html

105 https://rewire.news/article/2018/02/25/failed-students-parkland-also-failed-nikolas-cruz

What About Mental Health?

106 http://www.dcf.state.fl.us/newsroom/publicdocuments/Headquarters/Records20180219/2016-271667_Redacted%20per%20court%20order%20dated%202.19.18.pdf

107 https://www.npr.org/sections/health-shots/2018/03/06/591141401/mental-health-funding-tied-to-floridas-controversial-gun-legislation

108 http://wlrn.org/post/senate-passes-bill-crafted-response-parkland-scaled-down-program-arming-school-staff

109 https://www.npr.org/2017/10/03/555361499/did-the-las-vegas-shooter-use-a-device-that-helped-him-fire-faster

110 http://thehill.com/policy/healthcare/374304-dems-say-gop-focus-on-mental-health-is-redirection-from-gun-control

111 http://behaviorismandmentalhealth.com/2014/09/22/mass-murderers-and-psychiatric-drugs

112 https://www.cchrint.org/2018/02/20/school-shootings-mental-health-watchdog-says-psychotropic-drug-use-by-school-shooters-merits-federal-investigation

113 https://www.scientificamerican.com/article/should-children-take-antipsychotic-drugs

114 http://www.politico.com/story/2013/10/us-mass-shootings-tripled-098617

115 http://journals.plos.org/plosone/article?id=10.1371/journal.pone.0015337

116 https://www.nytimes.com/2018/02/15/us/gun-access-mentally-ill.html

117 http://www.wlns.com/news/6-news-on-demand/skubick-red-flag-law-touches-off-controversy-at-capitol/1036157215

118 https://www.aclu.org/blog/mobilization/aclus-position-gun-control

119 http://www.riaclu.org/news/post/aclu-of-rhode-island-raises-red-flags-over-red-flag-gun-legislation

120 http://www.fox4news.com/news/schools-revisit-security-concerns-after-santa-fe-hs-shooting

121 https://www.cnn.com/2018/03/14/us/ryan-petty-walk-up-walk-out-stoneman-douglas-shooting-trnd/index.html

122 https://www.nytimes.com/2018/03/27/opinion/nikolas-cruz-shooting-florida.html

123https://www.facebook.com/UnderreportedTheDailySignal/videos/391676421335394

124 http://www.businessinsider.com/schools-are-banning-best-friends-to-protect-kids-feelings-2017-9

125 https://onlinelibrary.wiley.com/doi/full/10.1111/cdev.12905

126 https://www.usnews.com/opinion/articles/2014/03/17/how-common-core-standards-kill-creative-teaching

127 https://www.washingtonpost.com/news/answer-sheet/wp/2015/02/20/a-superintendent-says-refusing-common-core-tests-is-dangerous-a-mom-says-hes-wrong/?noredirect=on&utm_term=.b899706ea777

128 https://www.npr.org/sections/ed/2016/01/03/460254858/turns-out-monkey-bars-and-kickball-are-good-for-the-brain

129 https://www.today.com/parents/want-kids-listen-more-fidget-less-try-more-recess-school-t65536

130 https://liinkproject.tcu.edu

The Breakdown of The American Family & A Disconnection From The Real World

131 https://www.cnn.com/2015/11/03/us/minnesota-foiled-school-massacre-john-ladue/index.html

132 http://www.sciencemag.org/news/2013/11/why-teenagers-are-so-impulsive

133 https://www.npr.org/sections/theprotojournalist/2013/09/24/225689775/why-are-most-rampage-shooters-men

134 https://www.ncbi.nlm.nih.gov/pubmed/23763107

135 http://www.misc.com.au/mhirc/docs/Munro%20Jonathan.pdf

136 http://extras.denverpost.com/news/shot0429b.htm

137 https://www.cnn.com/2015/06/19/us/charleston-church-shooting-suspect/index.html

138 http://www.newsweek.com/why-young-kill-166890

139 https://www.psychologytoday.com/us/blog/putting-psyche-back-psychotherapy/201510/are-you-spiritual-or-religious-does-it-matter

140 http://ftp.iza.org/dp5215.pdf

141 https://www.livescience.com/1465-study-religion-good-kids.html

142 https://www.psychologytoday.com/us/blog/nurturing-resilience/201406/does-religion-make-children-resilient

143 http://psycnet.apa.org/record/2013-13053-002

144 http://www.abc.net.au/news/2015-06-25/study-finds-heavy-metal-reduces-anger-depression/6571820

145 Farrell, Warren and Gray, John. *The Boy Crisis: Why Our Boys Are Struggling and What We Can Do About It.* BenBella Books, 2018.

146 http://dailycaller.com/2016/06/17/republicans-should-man-up-on-fatherlessness

147 http://thefederalist.com/2015/07/14/guess-which-mass-murderers-came-from-a-fatherless-home

148 http://onlinesense.org/4-ways-protect-kids-online-after-divorce

149 http://www.foxnews.com/opinion/2014/09/26/plugged-in-and-tuned-out-how-to-handle-teenage-virtual-addiction.html

150 https://www.nationalreview.com/2017/07/teen-suicides-depression-anxiety-rising-religion-can-help

151 https://www.psychologytoday.com/blog/out-the-darkness/201307/the-power-purpose

Can We Avoid Slippery Slopes?

[152] https://www.usatoday.com/story/opinion/2018/05/25/santa-fe-parkland-school-shooting-parents-arne-duncan-boycott-column/641548002

[153] http://webserver.rilin.state.ri.us/billtext18/housetext18/h7075aaa.htm

[154] https://reason.com/archives/2018/05/14/assault-weapons-explained

[155] https://www.opensecrets.org/lobby/top.php?indexType=l&showYear=2017

[156] https://www.opensecrets.org/lobby/top.php?indexType=c&showYear=2017

[157] https://www.opensecrets.org/lobby/top.php?indexType=u&showYear=2017

[158] https://www.opensecrets.org/lobby/top.php?indexType=i&showYear=2017

[159] http://ij.org/activism/legislation/civil-forfeiture-legislative-highlights

[160] https://theoutline.com/post/3571/david-hogg-parkland-interview?zd=5&zi=6ilwb6bn

[161] https://www.youtube.com/watch?time_continue=237&v=RIRNURx1-3E

[162] http://www.ilga.gov/legislation/fulltext.asp?DocName=10000HB1465hamo01&GA=100&SessionId=91&DocTypeId=HB&LegID=101955&DocNum=1465&GAID=14&Session

[163] https://www.americanthinker.com/articles/2018/03/gun_confiscation_begins_in_illinois.html

[164] http://insider.foxnews.com/2018/06/05/deerfield-illinois-weapons-ban-state-rifle-association-fights-back

[165] https://www.youtube.com/watch?v=xljj9OCgIXw

[166] https://www.washingtontimes.com/news/2018/may/27/publix-suspends-political-donations-after-die-in-p

[167] https://www.npr.org/sections/thetwo-way/2018/02/28/589436112/dicks-sporting-goods-ends-sale-of-assault-style-rifles-citing-florida-shooting

[168] https://mobile.nytimes.com/2015/08/27/business/walmart-to-end-sales-of-assault-rifles-in-us-stores.html

[169] https://www.reuters.com/article/us-usa-guns-lawsuits/oregon-man-20-sues-walmart-dicks-over-raising-gun-buying-age-idUSKCN1GI2CG

[170] https://www.politico.com/story/2017/12/05/gay-wedding-cake-supreme-court-280944

[171] https://www.youtube.com/watch?v=RgWIhYAtan4

[172] https://www.nytimes.com/2018/06/04/us/politics/supreme-court-sides-with-baker-who-turned-away-gay-couple.html

[173] http://www.kcra.com/article/bay-area-coffee-shop-wont-serve-police-for-safety-of-customers/19299705

[174] https://www.washingtonpost.com/news/made-by-history/wp/2017/08/16/who-are-the-antifa/?utm_term=.54b786f47f6e

[175] https://www.theguardian.com/commentisfree/2017/nov/29/donald-trump-britain-first-fascist-sympathiser

[176] https://www.theatlantic.com/magazine/archive/2017/03/how-to-build-an-autocracy/513872

When Is Enough, Enough?

[177] https://www.cnn.com/2018/05/21/us/texas-santa-fe-school-shooting/index.html

[178] https://www.cbsnews.com/news/santa-fe-high-school-shooting-suspect-idd-as-dimitrios-pagourtzis-live-updates-today-2018-5-18

[179] http://www.dailymail.co.uk/news/article-5751333/Family-murdered-teen-reveal-Santa-Fe-High-School-gunman-pestered-daughter-dates.html

[180] https://www.khou.com/video/news/crime/student-teacher-pulled-fire-alarm-to-alert-rest-of-school-to-shooting/285-8132949

[181] https://www.chron.com/news/houston-texas/texas/article/Explosives-in-Santa-Fe-shooting-were-functional-12929376.php

[182] https://twitter.com/NYGovCuomo/status/997527474400571392

[183] https://twitter.com/GabbyGiffords/status/997531853803474944

[184] https://reason.com/blog/2018/05/18/gun-rights-gun-control-advocates-react-t

[185] https://twitter.com/davidhogg111/status/997504642991968256

[186] https://gun.laws.com/shotguns/sawed-off-shotgun

[187] http://www.wandtv.com/story/38225611/governor-father-owned-guns-used-in-texas-shooting

[188] https://soundcloud.com/conservativereview/mark-levin-interviews-texas-lt-gov-dan-patrick-on-santa-fe-high-school-shooting

[189] https://www.nytimes.com/2018/05/20/us/texas-school-shooting-guns.html

[190] https://www.cnn.com/2018/05/18/us/student-on-texas-school-shooting/index.html

[191] https://www.facebook.com/ChiefArtAcevedo/posts/1676298439150998

[192] https://www.mrctv.org/videos/msnbc-reporter-suggests-texas-teens-have-responsibility-become-voices-gun-reform

[193] http://www.apa.org/news/press/releases/2016/08/media-contagion.aspx

---

194 https://www.psychologytoday.com/us/blog/media-spotlight/201605/can-celebrity-suicides-lead-copycat-deaths

195 https://twitter.com/AndrewPollackFL/status/1002156158868697089

A Path Forward

196 https://www.nytimes.com/2017/09/24/opinion/dying-art-of-disagreement.html

www.ingramcontent.com/pod-product-compliance
Lightning Source LLC
Chambersburg PA
CBHW070130260726
48658CB00001B/346